Praᴫ

"This book is a much-needed gift to the magical and energy work community. Sophie Reicher not only recognizes the need for better psychic protection from others, but our own need to protect others from our abilities. Thank you, Sophie, for sharing your skills with those willing to read and learn."

—Ruth Fishman, First Kingdom Church of Asphodel

"This book is a necessary addition to any spiritual bookshelf, regardless of individual path. All too often, basic skills such as grounding, centering, cleansings, and wardings are covered by authors in a few scant pages. In this essential guide, Reicher finally treats these key skills with the depth and insight they deserve. The instructions are clear enough for a beginner but with enough thoughtful information that even a seasoned practitioner can learn a thing or two."

—Anya Kless, author of *Lilith: Queen of the Desert*

Spiritual
Protection

SPIRITUAL PROTECTION

A Safety Manual for Energy Workers,
Healers, and Psychics

By Sophie Reicher

This edition first published in 2010 by New Page Books, an imprint of
Red Wheel/Weiser, LLC
With offices at:
65 Parker Street, Suite 7
Newburyport, MA 01950
www.redwheelweiser.com
www.newpagebooks.com

ISBN: 978-1-60163-124-4

Library of Congress Cataloging-in-Publication Data
Reicher, Sophie.
    Spiritual protection : a safety manual for energy workers, healers, and
psychics / by Sophie Reicher.
        p. cm.
    Includes bibliographical references (p.) and index.
    ISBN 978-1-60163-124-4 -- ISBN 978-1-60163-725-3 (ebook)
        1. Self-defense--Psychic aspects I. Title.
BF1045.S46R45 2010
133.8--dc22

                                                            2010018966

Cover design by Dutton & Sherman
Interior by Diana Ghazzawi

Printed in the United States of America
IBI
10   9   8   7   6   5   4   3   2   1

To Fuensanta Arismendi Plaza (1950–2010)

Although she was not a magician or energy-worker (in fact, she rather fervently hated magic), she was an astonishingly gracious, kind, and compassionate woman. She was also the most devoted servant of her Gods (Loki, Sigyn, Narvi, Vali, and Andvari) I have ever met, and everyone who encountered her walked away transformed by her commitment to Them. Without ever realizing it, she taught many of us more about devotion, humility, and service to our Gods than she herself would ever have believed. In her, it was as if an echo of Sigyn walked in our midst and in our world. She will be well and sorely missed.

Disclaimer

The author and the publisher disclaim any liability arising directly or indirectly from the use of this book. The author will not accept any responsibility for any omissions, misinterpretations, or misstatements that may exist within this book. The author is not engaged in rendering medical services. This book should not be construed as medical advice, nor should it take the place of regular scheduled appointments with a health-care professional. No warranty, express or implied, is delivered by the author or publisher with respect to the contents of this work.

Contents

Preface

Training psychic gifts has been part and parcel of my life for nearly 20 years. It began out of the sheer need to find a way to survive, to understand what was happening to me as my own very strong gift of empathy developed. Long before I ever practiced magic or any type of energy-work, I used that particular talent. I didn't have a choice—I was born with it, and it only got stronger with age. Those born with the proclivity for certain psychic talents find the world a far different place than those who are "head blind" or psi-null. To an empath, for instance, the world is a battleground of conflicting emotions, all of which pummel them with the force of physical blows. To the telepath, it is a jarring, loud confusion of noise that never stops. And to the seer, it is a confusing whir of color and images, people and experiences, possibilities and potentialities to which the average person is blind. Learning how to manage and control these gifts is not simply the indulgence of a fanatical New-Ager; rather it's a matter of pure survival.

After nearly two decades of teaching students to use and control their psi-talents, I am thoroughly convinced that a sizeable percentage of people on psychiatric medications and even those who are institutionalized would benefit from this type of training. I long ago lost count of the students who came to me wanting to know if they were going crazy. Some had tried going to a therapist or psychiatrist for help, only to find that the "help" provided did no good at all, whereas learning to actively use and control their gifts did. Nearly all had been diagnosed with clinical depression and all of them suffered high levels of anxiety and stress. Now this is not to say that every single person under a psychiatrist's care is really psychic; that would be going too far. I am simply saying that strong, untrained gifts can cause a person to doubt his or her own sanity. Unfortunately, even when they do seek out help from a mental health profession, unless they are very, very fortunate, most professionals are unprepared to credit their experiences with any degree of truth and are therefore unable to provide effective help. We simply don't live in a culture that understands these things. They are regarded as outré, arcane, fanciful, and even dangerous.

Unfortunately, they are not necessarily fanciful to those who actually possess these talents. Whereas most people experience the world through a sensorium comprised solely of sight, sound, smell, taste, and touch, those with psi-gifts have the pressure of at least one additional sense to contend with, and that sense can make the world a confusing and sometimes unbearable place. Now these talents can be immensely valuable to the individual him- or herself and, in some cases, to his or her community. They have the potential to enhance one's life, but if and only if they're properly trained. Sadly, even in occult communities such training can be very difficult to find. I was fortunate: I stumbled upon a series of novels that dealt fairly accurately with the gifts, as well as some occult literature from the early 20th century that offered solid, practical suggestions for basic training exercises—works such as those of Dion Fortune, Denning and Phillips, and Israel Regardi. Later I found a very skilled and blessedly ethical teacher. When I first became Pagan in the early 1990s (which also coincided with my beginning the practice of energy-work), these authors were still occasionally being discussed. Within a decade, however, they had fallen almost completely out of favor. It is surprising today to find newcomers to the Pagan community—and worse, to the occult or energy-work community—who have heard of Fortune, let alone read her work. Newcomers would rather read just about anything than serious writing on occult theory.[1] To make matters even worse, if such a thing is possible, the current literature out there on anything approaching psychic self-defense all too often provides inaccurate and even dangerous information (white light, ladies and gentlemen, is not a cure-all).

There have been some very good and useful books published in the last decade, despite my own rather grim account of the state of the community. Some of these are listed in the Bibliography at the end of this book. The problem as I see it is that this training is no longer *de rigueur*, and what is on the market tends to be tradition-specific. Sloppiness and misinformation abounds. I believe there are many reasons for this, not the least of which is the fact that psi-gifts aren't bestowed equally among the population. Whether or not one has a specific talent depends far more on genetics than personal worthiness. There's nothing egalitarian about it, and that often doesn't sit well with many Pagan and/or New Age communities. I also think that we live in an age of instant gratification, and actively training the gifts or coaxing a latent gift to open takes much more hard work and (Gods forbid) discipline than the average person is willing to expend. It's much more gratifying to indulge in feel-good metaphysics that have little or no effective application in the physical world. Your average person can afford to do so; those who actually have psi-talents cannot.

The exercises that I present here are essential not only to learning to control one's gifts, but to learning effective, ethical, and safe energy-work. As a practicing magician, I've also chosen to address techniques that can help ward against magical attack. Although they are not the primary focus of this book, the exercises provided are simple enough that even the most elementary practitioner can learn to use them effectively. Because those with psi-talents are likely to also have some sensitivity to magic and magical energies, it seems only sensible to touch on a few basic precautions that can be taken to guarantee safety, both of oneself and one's home. By the way, there's no reason why a person without psi-talent (and totally uninterested in developing it) couldn't find some benefit in the basic exercises given in this book. They're excellent tools both for meditation and for increasing one's receptivity to spiritual forces. Many of the basic exercises aid in stilling the mind and in learning to sense energy, including the energy of a Deity's presence. More importantly, I have used them to combat one of the most devastating diseases of modern life: stress. These exercises, particularly those for grounding and centering, are for everyone, because stress is a killer—literally. It's also blocked energy, which is just the thing that these techniques prevent.

Ultimately, it is my hope in writing this book that I'll be providing my readers with the type of book that I desperately longed for as a teenager and young adult, and continue to long for even now, when one of my students asks for good basic reading material. In these pages, I share 20 years of personal experience in training psi-talents, in learning to control and master my own, and in learning effective energy-work. The exercises given in this book are useful on many fronts, and not just for the psychic. They are also indispensable for the occult-ist or practicing magician, and for the Pagan or Heathen wish-ing to develop either ritual skills or a devotional practice. There is much crossover in applicability. If this book spares even one reader the pain and struggle that I myself went through, then I have done my job.

1

The Fundamentals

We're going to begin with the most basic and utterly essential exercises for anyone interested in developing their gifts, engaging in devotional practice, learning to practice magic, or learning to work with energy. Regardless of whether you are a practicing magician, a Pagan, or a Heathen, pretty much everyone can benefit from these exercises. If you interact with people in any way, shape, or form during the day, you will at some point be influenced by their energy and emotional state. We relate to people through the emotional connections engendered by our interactions, whether we are consciously aware of it or not. It's part of being human. Physics tells us that everything is comprised of energy in motion. *We* are made up of energy in motion, and those daily interactions with friends, family members, coworkers, and the stranger on the street are, essentially, intersecting bodies of energy. That intersection can bring about a type of energy contamination.

Unless we have the gift of Sight we can't generally see such energy, but we can't see germs with the naked eye either, yet no one disputes their ability to affect us. Energy is everywhere and in everything. Emotions, for example, are energy: How many times have you walked into a room in which two people have just had a terrible argument and felt the pall in the room? Perhaps it made you uncomfortable or agitated. This is normal. Whether we want them to or not, our bodies respond to such unseen stimuli, even if we are otherwise generally psi-null. They can affect our mood and our stress levels, even our overall health. The exercises given in this chapter can help mitigate the effects of such psychic contamination. This is your first line of defense against imbalances in the etheric body and the first positive step you can take in maintaining a healthy psyche and physical body. Etheric imbalances can eventually affect one's physical and mental health. In part this occurs because energetic imbalances create stress, which can disrupt the body's equilibrium, leading to a plethora of physical maladies. This is one of the reasons why many of these exercises are equally helpful in times of emotional upset and turmoil, and why all of them are excellent stress reducers. For those who may be psychically talented, they are an absolute necessity.

In many respects these basic exercises are like a martial arts *kata*. When one practices kata in a martial arts class, the structured movements reinforce every technique that one is learning. Many of the forms were passed down, largely unchanged, from generation to generation. They train both the mind and body, developing a kinetic memory and slowly strengthening the muscles and reflexes. The discipline of consistent practice builds a physical foundation that eventually enables the martial artist to adapt and function in any circumstance. It leads to a tremendous freedom and fluidity of execution. These basic psychic exercises do exactly the same thing: they hone and strengthen mental and intuitive abilities and put you in control of your gifts rather than the other way around. They also help you manage the potentially overwhelming stimuli that constantly bombard us from every quarter, whether we are psychic or not. We are beings of energy—molecules in motion—and these techniques provide basic survival skills for keeping that energy in top form.

As with medicine, an ounce of prevention is worth a pound of cure, so before we delve into the realm of advanced energy-work, shielding and warding, attack and counter-attack, it's necessary to first master those exercises that will prevent 99 percent of most esoteric harm, including the harm we do to ourselves from lack of common sense.

Centering and Grounding

The most important exercises one can do, whether to develop one's gifts, manage stress, or begin one's devotional practice, are centering and grounding. These two exercises go hand-in-hand and are the backbone of any spiritual, magical, or energetic practice. They still the mind, make one aware of the flow of energy in one's body, provide control over that energy, and, in the end, bring an inner stillness that allows one to hear the voice of the Gods. They also make one exquisitely aware of one's psychic, emotional, and physical boundaries and help lay the foundation for effective psychic and energy shields.

Centering and grounding are the most essential exercises you will ever learn. Ideally they should be done at least once a day, preferably twice. I generally recommend a minimum of 15 minutes in the morning and another 15 minutes right before bed. Checking one's ground throughout the day at regular intervals is not a bad idea either, especially for the novice. In fact, I often tell students to use a mnemonic: for instance, every time you see something red, you'll check your ground; or every time you see a silver car, you'll check your shields. Eventually, after many years of doing these exercises, you can reduce that frequency to once or twice a day, but in the beginning there's no such thing as too much self-evaluation.

There are numerous ways to go about both centering and grounding. I tend to start people off with breathing exercises. The most common of these tend to involve visualizations, but not many people (empaths included) can visualize well. For those just starting out, struggling with exercises that go against one's preferred learning modality can seem like an almost insurmountable obstacle to excellence. For that reason and for general practicality, I prefer to start people off with something a little more kinetic. I am a very kinetic learner who was constantly frustrated by the emphasis on visual techniques when I first started out. That experience taught me that there are many different ways to process energy, something that we will be discussing a little further on in the book. Although I provide only a few examples of grounding and centering, it should be noted that there are many different ways to go about both exercises. The important thing is to do them regularly.

I was taught that centering should be done before grounding.[1] Centering basically means making sure that your physical, etheric/astral, and auric bodies all occupy exactly the same space.[2] This has to be done before the energy channels in the body can be properly aligned to best facilitate grounding. Centering is not difficult. The first exercise (and the one that I consider to be the best) is one that I originally learned in a martial arts class. It has many uses and, best of all, it is very, very simple. All that is necessary is a purposeful focus on your breathing. Taking slow, even breaths, inhale four counts, hold four counts, exhale four counts, and hold four counts. That's all. Do it over and over again, repeating the pattern without breaks. Don't rush—try to feel your breath filling your entire body. Try timing it to your heartbeat (if that's too distracting don't worry about it and just breathe). In time, as you breathe, you want to feel all the breath, all the excess, scattered, or jangled energy in your body, gathering about three inches below your naval. This is your second chakra.

A chakra is a nexus of energy in the body. The word comes from the Sanskrit for "wheel." Unless we have the gift of Sight we can't see chakras, but they affect the overall energy of our body. I believe that they are the energetic equivalent of nerve ganglia, points of confluence where several meridians or energy lines converge. There are seven major chakras and many other minor ones. Most energy-workers concentrate on these seven, sometimes adding the palms of the hands, through which energy may be channeled. Although not everyone works with chakras, I'm partial to them because the very first centering exercise I ever learned involved chakra work.

Returning to the centering exercise, as you breathe, you eventually want to feel and/or see the energy gathering in a glowing golden ball at this chakra. Basically, centering is, quite literally, contemplating your naval. Be sure to breathe using your diaphragm, taking deep, even breaths. If you do not yet trust your ability to either see or feel the energy you're working with, don't worry: imagine the energy flowing where you wish it to flow. Imagination is an important tool for learning to work with energy, and it can be a powerful key to unlocking and developing one's sensitivities. By indulging your imagination and purposefully wielding it, you're giving your subconscious tacit permission to acknowledge not only your creativity but any hidden sensitivities to energy, as well. It's a nice way of circumventing the internal censor we all have. You know that censor—the little voice inside that says this is ridiculous, stupid, or silly, or that you aren't good enough, talented enough, and so on. Half of developing competence with psi-gifts or energy-work is learning to ignore and eventually silence that inner critic.

Centering can be very calming when you are under stress. If you find yourself in an emotionally stressful situation, it may help to engage in this breathing pattern. Of all the ways there are to center, this tends to be the easiest and most adaptable. One's center is based on where one's center of gravity is. For most women, this is somewhere in the abdomen, the second chakra area. Larger women and most men center at the solar plexus or in some cases even higher. I don't recommend using anything but the second or third chakra for this exercise, though.

The purpose of centering is to align your energy body with your physical body and to make sure they both have the same shape and spatial boundaries. It's also about being fully present in your body.[3] We're incarnated for a reason. Our bodies are an important part of our spiritual process; they are the conduit through which we experience everything. Far from being something that we should dismiss or ignore, our physical body—our sensorium—is a powerful and sacred spiritual tool. This is especially so for energy-workers. Be aware of the physical and emotional sensations that these exercises may trigger. Both centering and grounding prepare the body for a free, healthy, unclogged flow of internal energy. Sometimes when energy blocks are removed, there can be physical and emotional side effects. Both physical tension and emotions are, after all, energy.

Once the excess energy in your body has been collected it has to go somewhere. Grounding adds stability by providing one's energy matrix with a connection to the earth. Basically, grounding is sending all that excess energy that has been collected down into the earth. By doing so, it provides both a stabilizing system of energetic "roots," and a "shunt" for excess energies in the body. It also creates a "tap root" through which one can replenish one's energies when they run low. In my opinion, this is even more important than centering. We can function without being properly centered—look at the world around us; people do it all the time. However, if one's ground is fully blocked it can cause severe illness. Most people instinctively have at least some sort of connection like this. It may not be strong or open or consciously created, but it's part of the body's energetic physiology, just as a functioning liver is part of the body's physical physiology. It's always better and more effective, however, if one is actively working one's ground. After all, we have to eat right and exercise and get enough sleep for our physical bodies to remain healthy; likewise, for our energetic bodies to remain in good condition, a little active care is necessary there, too. Instinct isn't enough to keep these channels open, healthy, and functioning properly.

Grounding is occasionally boring, but it's not difficult. The basic and most common grounding exercise is a good one. It entails feeling a cord of energy extending from your root chakra down into the earth, reaching deeper and deeper and rooting you strongly. What most people won't tell you is that the cord should be a double conduit: one half allows you to send energy down, while the other allows you to draw energy up. Alternately, you can create two separate cords, which will do the same thing. There's a reason for this that comes into play if you are doing an extensive amount of energy-work. If you get hit with an excessive amount of energy, you need to be able to "dump" it through that shunt very quickly, or you'll get what's called a "reaction headache." You can't do that if you're using a one-way cord. It creates the energetic equivalent of a clogged pipe, so keep that in mind as you learn the following exercise.[4]

The easiest exercise to begin with involves controlling one's breathing. Inhale and feel the energy gathered in your center. As you exhale, feel that energy exiting the body through the perineum. On the second exhale, feel it entering the earth and branching out into a thick, sturdy network of roots. I usually visualize this energy as a gold cord and a network of fluid and flexible gold roots. Embrace this imagery for as long as you need to, with each ensuing exhalation taking you further and further into the earth until you feel fully grounded. Although you can ground in multiple places (and this will be discussed a little further on in this book), the most important ground of all is the one here in the physical world—what Northern Traditionalists such as myself call Midgard. Ground your awareness and energy cord right into the soil, into the land on which you're sitting, standing, or walking. You have a right to this ground. You have a right to the connection to this soil. It is yours by right of birth. Knowing that to be true in the marrow of your bones makes this process a thousand times easier. It is this awareness that must inform your grounding. You are engaging in and claiming that which is yours by right. Right of ownership is a powerful thing in magic and other types of energy-work. It's a difficult claim to challenge, so putting yourself in that position can make your ground that much more solid.

Many occult books, particularly ones that speak in depth about astral projection, discuss a silver cord that attaches the soul to the body and which can sometimes be seen when one astrally projects. The grounding cord that one creates through the previous exercise is just as vital. You may have heard of that well-known and ancient occult maxim, "as above, so below." Thus, the grounding cord is the natural complement to the astral/etheric cord. The physical world is just as important as the spiritual. Rather than being diametrically opposed to one another, they should function together like two halves of a balanced whole.

When you eventually learn different ways of grounding, you will find that many of the exercises are primarily visualization exercises. Don't worry if you're not adept at visualizing things; that too is a skill that comes in time. I personally struggled with this for many years. You may find that images come via feelings instead of sight, and that's fine. Don't worry if you can't see or feel anything—start with the mental focus, and eventually your awareness of the internal flow of energy will increase. Energy follows awareness, and awareness follows imagination disciplined to will. Create the "groove" in your mind through daily, repetitive practice and eventually that groove will be created in fact, in one's energy, and in one's astral and etheric bodies.

I learned a simple breathing exercise that can help with grounding from my first teacher, who wasn't particularly visually oriented, either. For this exercise, inhale four counts, exhale six counts, and hold six counts. Repeat this for as long as necessary. This can be very effective if you are having difficulty grounding. I cannot emphasize enough that this is the most important exercise you will ever learn as an energy-worker. I have had people say to me, "I don't want to ground, I just want to do Reiki," or "I don't want to ground, I just want to heal." Well, if you're not grounded, you're not doing squat. In fact, if you're not grounded and you engage in energy-work, in my opinion (and that of every competent energy-worker I know), you're engaging in something unethical, foolish, and potentially dangerous, both to yourself and your client.

As an aside, I've often found it difficult to ground in air-planes and trains. I tend to be fairly literal about some things, and I can't help but get distracted by the image of my ground-ing roots running with me or stretching to accommodate a plane. Silly, yes, but very distracting, too! My colleagues and good friends from Clan Tashlin taught me a specific grounding to combat this; they refer to it as the "Little Prince exercise." Picture yourself standing upon the planet earth. See yourself as very small, the size of an ant, and surrounded and engulfed by the enormous, massive body of the earth itself. You should try to imagine yourself in proper scale in relation to the mas-sive size of the planet. If you can put yourself into that experi-ence viscerally, it will automatically ground you strongly and effectively.

On an amusing side note, as one of my former students once said (with more than a little exasperation), grounding is similar to "peeing out" what bothers you. You gather all the upsetting, jagged, excessive energy in your body and send it out through the root. Gather all toxins that may have come from without, including negative emotions, and energetically pee them out. That's grounding.

In addition to meditation and visualization techniques, it is also possible to use natural substances, such as stones and herbs, to ground. This should not in any way take the place of regular grounding practice. It is a stop-gap technique to use in times of extreme need. One of the best grounding stones I know of is hematite. It is absolutely one of the strongest grounding stones I have ever encountered. Tiger iron also works very well, but I tend to favor hematite as it is somewhat more readily avail-able. Energy-wise, it's very dense and heavy, which makes it the ideal tool to focus on for a student who is having problems grounding. (I have one student who cannot use this stone, for it is so dense that she feels suffocated when she links into its en-ergy.) All living things have energy, and that energy resonates at different frequencies. By aligning one's internal energies with that of a specific stone or herb, one can bring about the desired change—for example, using hematite for grounding.

A good meditation is to sit, holding a chosen stone in one's hand, and, while focusing one's breath into the stone, slowly align one's internal energies to the stone's frequency. Everyone has trouble grounding and centering from time to time, but this exercise can help alleviate some of those problems. Just sit and breathe, concentrating on how the stone feels and how it makes you feel when you hold it. Notice temperature, weight, emotions, images—anything that comes to mind. If you're having trouble grounding, or if you know you're going to be going into an emotionally or energetically charged situation, I recommend carrying or wearing a piece of hematite. It's a good reminder of what it feels like to be solidly and completely grounded.

Another use for hematite (or any stone, actually), and one that is seldom mentioned in occult books anymore, is in making elixirs by imbuing tea or water with the qualities of the stone. It's one way of internally cleansing what a spiritual bath or rubdown would take care of externally.[5] It can be used in conjunction with the techniques given previously to aid in grounding or any other working. I would not use it by itself, and again, it is not a substitute for regular practice. Obviously some degree of knowledge about herbs is required for safety's sake. I would suggest taking a class in medicinal herbology, or picking up either *Grieve's Herbal* or the *PDR for Herbal Medicines* as a reference. Following are two simple recipes for a grounding elixir. One part equals about one teaspoon.

୭ Grounding Elixir #1 ୭

- ୭ 2 parts dandelion
- ୭ 1 part violet
- ୭ 1 part yarrow
- ୭ 1 part red clover

Pour boiling water over the herbs and allow the elixir to sit for roughly 20 minutes. Strain it into a bottle. Place a piece of hematite into the bottle and let sit for at least 24 hours in the refrigerator. A glass of this elixir may be drunk whenever you practice your grounding. If you are planning on keeping this for a long time, make a tincture rather than an infusion. This is done by allowing the herbs to sit in a bottle of high-proof vodka for a minimum of six weeks before straining. Tinctures need not be refrigerated and will keep for months. Typically, when making tinctures, one part equals one ounce of the requisite herbs.

Herbal medicines can also be prepared by tincture and/or infusion, but magical elixirs are not meant to be used for medicinal purposes.

୭ Grounding Elixir #2 ୭

- ୭ 2 parts red clover
- ୭ 1 part ginseng
- ୭ 1 part betony
- ୭ 1 tiger iron stone

Make an elixir as directed above. Wait at least 24 hours before using. Again, none of these elixirs or stones substitute in any way for daily grounding and centering.

Reaction Sickness

One of the reasons that grounding and centering are so important to psychics, energy-workers, and magicians is that they prevent and protect against something called reaction sickness. This is caused by one of three things: overworking oneself in psi-work, energy-work, or magic; suddenly being bombarded with too much energy too quickly; or expending too much energy too quickly, which can cause the same unpleasant effect. Reaction sickness is a sign that the body's energy channels have been completely overloaded. It can result in terrible headaches (even migraines), nausea, dizziness, sore muscles, and, in extreme cases, shock. Having a good, solid ground is the best means of prevention. Most students experience this at least once in their training. How will you know when you are experiencing it? The milder forms can be a response to overworking the gifts. Energy overload, which can lead to reaction headaches, can also manifest as hyperactivity and giddiness rather than exhaustion and nausea. Be on the lookout for either response.

If you are dealing with someone in the throes of reaction sickness, or if you have fallen prey to this yourself (and it happens to the best of us), there are a few things you can do to start the healing process. First, ground yourself using any of the techniques discussed in this book. If you can get outside and connect to trees and the earth itself, that can help immensely, too. Walk barefoot or sit directly on the ground or with your back against a tree. There's something to the whole idea of hugging a tree that one hears occasionally from New Agers.

Eat something, preferably protein. I often find that I crave sugar when this happens, which has lead me to believe that reaction sickness disrupts not only the body's electrolytes but also blood-sugar levels. I keep a protein bar, chocolate, and some sort of energy drink in my kit when I work. Make sure you're hydrated, and take ibuprofen or aspirin if you have a headache. The effects of energy sickness can last for days in the worst cases, and there's nothing quite as annoying as having a hangover when you haven't had anything alcoholic to drink. That is what this type of sickness is like in many cases. Take the aspirin. Get a massage if possible, or take a bath into which you've put a grounding elixir or beer (we will discuss beer baths in the chapter on cleansing). Hold or wear heavy grounding stones. Finally, after you've done as many of these things as you can, go to bed and sleep until you wake up naturally.

Many serious energy-workers practice either qi gong, tai chi, yoga, or some form of martial arts. All of these things help you get in touch with your physicality and aid in developing a greater awareness of your internal energies. Plus, they can keep you healthy. For those that are serious about moving past psi-training and getting into active energy-work and/or magic, I highly recommend getting training in one of the aforementioned arts.

Quick-Fix Grounding Techniques

Although none of these quick-fix techniques substitute for daily, disciplined practice (I've yet to have a student who doesn't get bored with grounding long before it's truly mastered), sometimes emergencies happen, and you will need to ground more quickly than perhaps your skill will allow. Sometimes, too, circumstances intervene to make regular grounding difficult. Here are six things you can do to tide yourself over until you have the opportunity and ability to effectively ground, which should be done as soon as possible:

1. Have a full meal, preferably with a good deal of protein. Food and the process of digesting are, in and of themselves, mildly grounding.

2. Have someone pour a gallon of cold water over your head. This is unpleasant, but it will snap your awareness back into your physical body like nothing else. This is particularly effective if you are having trouble coming out of a trance. This is something to keep in mind for emergency situations. I've used it on people when they were having trouble coming back to themselves after intense ritual work that involved Deity possession.[6]

3. Bathe or shower and change clothes. This has much the same effect as the second option, but in a far less jolting way.

4. Have a more experienced person ground you. Some energy-workers and psychics have the ability to ground other people. It depends on their individual talents, but anyone with empathy or healing, and certainly any *psi-vamp* (psychic vampire), should be able to do this effectively.[7]

5. Some people find sex very grounding; for others it has the opposite effect. Use your best judgment here.

6. Some people find flogging or being smacked very grounding (think of slapping a hysterical person to bring him/her back to his/her senses). Again, for others it has the opposite effect. It's really helpful to know your body's responses and what will work best for you.

Chakras and How to Cleanse Them

This is a more elaborate method of centering, which I believe is generally good to do at least once a week. This exercise entails cleansing each of the seven main chakras and then aligning them for a free flow of energy. The very first meditation exercise I ever learned (given on pages 36–37) dealt with the chakras, and I've found nothing better for regular energy maintenance. There are numerous other chakra points in the body other than these seven, but when dealing with occult matters, it's the primary seven, which lie along the body's axis, that we are mostly concerned with. I occasionally perform this exercise incorporating the two chakras that lie above the crown and the two that lie below the root (one right between the feet in the energy body and one further down in the aura). Yes, the aura/etheric body has chakras, too! I don't know what these chakras are called (nor does anyone else I know) but they *are* there, and it's a good idea to work them once in a while. Once you've grown comfortable with the following exercise, feel free to do the same.

As I noted previously, there are seven main chakras in the body, and they can impact one's emotional, psychic, and physical health, and/or create blockages that can impact one's ability to perform energy-work and one's overall spiritual work. Therefore it is necessary to keep them clean and well-balanced. A lot of what I'm telling you in this section may be a bit overwhelming, but just do your best and eventually everything will click into place.

Following is a chart that provides correspondences for each of the chakras. This may help in your work with them. It's not necessary to memorize this; it's just helpful information to have. In time you'll discover your own correspondences. It's just helpful information to have. I have seen other, perhaps more traditional correspondences, but this is the system that I learned 20 years ago and the one in which I feel competent enough to teach. (Thanks to Galina Krasskova for her kind permission to use this chart, a version of which first appeared in her *Whisperings of Woden*, published by Asphodel Press.)

Chakra	Sanskrit Name	Location	Color	Stones	What it Governs	Element
Root chakra	Muldhara (foundation)	Perinium	Red	Hematite, ruby	Survival, vital life-force, material support, security, health	Earth
Sex chakra	Svidisthana or Hara (abode of vital force)	2 to 3 inches below the naval	Orange	Moonstone, carnelian, copper	Desire, self-image, self-confidence, sexuality, bladder, kidneys	Water
Solar plexus chakra	Manipuraka (seat of fire/jewel of the naval)	Below the breastbone	Yellow	Gold, tiger's eye, citrine	Self-mastery, will, motivation, anger	Fire
Heart chakra	Anahatha (unbeaten)	Center of the chest	Green, pink	Rose quartz, chryso-phrase, jade, watermelon tourmeline, malachite	Emotions, love, loss, compassion	Air
Throat chakra	Visshudha (pure)	Bottom of neck	Blue	Lapis, aquamarine	Expression, communi-cation	Sound
Third eye chakra	Ajna (command)	Between the brows	Indigo, white	Quartz, amethyst	Magic and psychic gifts	Ki (Chi)

Chakra	Sanskrit Name	Location	Color	Stones	What it Governs	Element
Crown	Sahasrara (thousand-petaled lotus)	Crown of the head	Purple	Sugilite, purple flourite	Wisdom, divine connection	Connection to divinity

The following exercise is a good way to clean the chakras, to hone one's visualization abilities, and increase one's sensitivity to internal energies. The chakras penetrate the entire body and have a front and a back, so when you do these exercises, be certain to inhale the energy in through the front of your body (the front of the chakra), and exhale through the back. If you like, you can expand upon this exercise by working up the front of the body and down the back. I have found that to be a particularly effective variation.

First, ground and center just as you did in the previous exercises. That's always the first step. Begin to focus on your root chakra. Inhale, drawing energy and breath in through the root. Imagine that you're actually breathing through this chakra. Then exhale, sending that energy of breath out. As you exhale, feel all the blockages and dreck that are clouding that chakra flow away with the breath. Ideally, the chakras should be precisely three inches in diameter—no more, no less. If this is the first time you're doing this exercise, or if you have been going through a particularly challenging time in your life, cleaning the chakras and widening or narrowing them to the proper size can take a bit of time. Try to be patient.

Continue this for about a dozen exhalations then begin to visualize a small seed of glowing red light pulsing in the center of the root chakra. With each inhalation, the red light grows brighter and larger until it finally fills the entire chakra, pulsing and whirling and spinning. If you still feel that the chakra isn't fully clean, you can feel this red light like fire, burning up and devouring all that isn't clean and pure within. (This step can be repeated with the different colors throughout this exercise.)

When you feel that this chakra is opened and cleansed, turn your attention to the second chakra, the sex chakra. Do exactly the same thing, but when you exhale, send the energy out through the back of the chakra. This time you will visualize a glowing orange light. Move up through all the chakras and continue this exercise until you reach the crown. Use the appropriate color for each chakra (yellow for the solar plexus, green for the heart, blue for the throat, indigo for the third eye, and royal purple for the crown). Once you have reached the crown, return your attention to the root. Inhale, drawing energy up from the earth and through the root. I usually visualize it as clean, powerful, golden energy. As you exhale, allow that energy to travel through the chakras and burst from the crown, cascading around you like the branches of a weeping willow tree. This energy flows back into the earth. Do this at least six times. Then do the reverse, pulling energy in through the crown and allowing it to travel down to the root and into the earth. Do this at least six times, as well. As above, so below, even in a basic exercise such as this one. Afterward, ground as much as you feel you need to and have a little something to eat.

I recommend doing this exercise sitting down, not lying down, so that you don't fall asleep. I find that we live in such a stressful and rushed society that sometimes sitting down to meditate is the only time we give ourselves permission to really relax. This can sometimes cause one to fall asleep during the exercise. If this happens, it's perfectly normal and okay. It means your body is telling you it probably needs the sleep. These exercises put us in touch with our bodies, and sometimes the first result of that "conversation" is that we realize how much we've been neglecting those bodies. So if you fall asleep during your meditation, that's okay. It usually means you've managed to relax, which is a good sign. Go to bed and try it again the next day.

Sometimes when you're doing extensive chakra work, certain emotional and psychological issues may come up that need to be addressed. The work itself opens the door to the possibility for healing, giving the higher self tacit permission to begin dredging up those uncomfortable issues we usually try to hide or ignore. The exercises will also make us more aware of our internal and emotional patterns. By the same token, those issues are sometimes mirrored in one's daily life, too, providing even more opportunities for resolution. Each chakra has its own set of associations, so it's pretty eay to predict which issues or challenges may arise. For example:

- Root chakra: survival issues; money issues; fear about having shelter or enough food; body issues, particularly issues with food.

- Sex chakra: intimacy issues (physical intimacy, not necessarily emotional); body image issues/eating disorders; attitudes regarding sex and sexuality; boundaries.

- Solar plexus chakra: anger management issues; problems with assertiveness; boundaries.

- Heart chakra: emotional intimacy issues; hurt; loneliness; fear.

- Throat chakra: issues regarding communication.

- Third eye chakra: boundary issues where one's psi-gifts are concerned.

- Crown chakra: spiritual issues.

There are specific things you can do while working on a specific chakra that can help in dealing with these issues. These are things that I personally have found helpful, but you may come up with other approaches and techniques that work equally well based on your own life experience, so please do not feel limited by my suggestions here:

- Root chakra: yoga; qi gong (this is good for all chakras actually); thoroughly cleaning one's house; taking a financial management/budgeting class; taking cooking classes (nourishment is the most basic aspect of the root chakra); taking up a hands-on skill or craft such as pottery (made from clay, which is a gift of the earth).

- Sex chakra: massage; regular masturbation; Tantric work[8]; aromatherapy; belly dancing; tai chi; learning to adorn and dress oneself well; taking pride in one's appearance as a means of honoring the body and one's physicality; anything that develops one's awareness and appreciation of one's physical senses.

- Solar plexus chakra: martial arts; pilates (which focuses on strengthening one's core muscles); yoga.

- Heart chakra: Tonglen meditation; massage; therapy; qi gong; music lessons.

- Throat chakra: singing/voice lessons; acting lessons; creative writing; anything that fosters communication and creativity.

- Third eye chakra: all the fundamental exercises in this chapter!

- Crown chakra: regular devotional work to a Deity or Deities; prayer; meditation.

Tension is such a vicious thing that very often the first exercise an occultist will give his or her student (at least in the circles I was moving in for most of my training) is for relaxation. I was given two, which I'll share with you here:

ೂ Relaxation Exercise #1 ೲ

Sit comfortably in a chair or lie down comfortably on your back. (A word of warning: It's probably best done sitting up, because every single time I've done it lying down in bed, I've fallen asleep before I've even reached my knees!) Starting at your toes and slowly working your way up through each muscle group, relax each individual body part: toes, top of feet, heels, ankles, shins, calves, behind the knees, hamstrings, quad muscles, groin, hips, stomach, lower back, middle back, upper back, fingers, hands, wrists, forearms, elbows, upper arms, armpits (believe it or not, working on a computer creates a tremendous amount of tension in the armpits), the muscles between the ribs, chest, sternum, back of neck, jaw, mouth, cheeks, forehead, top of head. This is how carefully focused this exercise is. Don't rush; really go into your body and try to locate each particular muscle group and feel it loosening and relaxing. Over time, this will teach you to become extremely body-aware. I find that people with a background in dance, martial arts, or yoga tend to find these exercises easier in the beginning. Working down from the head is sometimes very helpful because then you can end the exercise by purposefully grounding all the remaining tension into the earth. You're also less likely to fall asleep.

☙ Relaxation Exercise #2 ❧

Sit or lie down comfortably. Starting at your feet and working downward, tense up your feet. Hold for three seconds and then release, feeling all the tension releasing, too. Do this with your calves, thighs, groin, hips, back, hands, arms, shoulders, neck, and face. I don't find this as thorough as the first exercise, but it's much easier for people who don't have a background in some physical art or practice (such as dance or martial arts) and who may not be as in touch with their bodies. Again, it doesn't matter what exercise you use; what matters is that you relax. Tension is blocked energy, and blocked energy is uncomfortable and inefficient. It also attracts negative energy and pain.

Advanced Grounding Techniques

You've already learned a very basic grounding exercise. Now we're going to take it to the next level. There is much, much more to grounding than learning to be a tree, though that particular visualization is still, I believe, the best place to start. That said, such a simplistic exercise, while fine for a beginner, will not afford adequate protection from psychic or magical attack, nor will it serve one well in many modes of energy-work, including healing. Once the basic exercises have been mastered, it's time to expand the premise and find a ground more suitable for magic, magical combat, healing work, and extensive gift-work. This should not even be attempted until you've been grounding and centering for at least six months; indeed, it will be impossible unless you have mastered basic grounding and centering. Please, don't even try without first doing the necessary work.

When I was initially taught to ground, I was told that one's ground is a two-way channel, in which you can pull energy up just as easily as you can send energy down. I was also taught that this is a foundational practice in many forms of healing and energy-work. This is only partly true. It's actually best to have a ground into which you can "root" energy down and another, separate channel through which you can draw energy up. I also recommend establishing multiple shunts through which you can quickly disperse large amounts of incoming energy. You can quickly see why the metaphor of a root system of a tree is so effective. If you suddenly need to dump energy and your ground is already occupied with drawing energy up, you're in trouble. Energy backlash is a nasty thing. It can lead to electrolyte disruption, nausea, migraines, fainting, and even shock. It's best to avoid this whenever possible, which is one of the goals of good basic training. As you take these exercises to the next level, your ground should be multifaceted, with at least one channel being used specifically to draw energy back into the body.

I'm a Northern Traditionalist, so I tend to default to Norse cosmology in my work. Feel free to adapt this exercise to your own cosmology. We're initially taught to ground in the earth of Midgard, deep into the land we stand upon, and this is the most essential ground one can establish. For stability and safety, it's very important that this be established first, before any other kind of ground. I would go so far as to say work regularly, even daily, for at least a year using only a Midgard ground. Once you have created a solid ground in the earth, begin working on grounding in two places at once: in the earth itself and, perhaps, at Yggdrasil, the World-Tree.

Norse cosmology has nine worlds:

1. Asgard: world of the Aesir.

2. Vanaheim: world of the Vanir.

3. Jotunheim: world of the Jotnar.

4. Alfheim: world of the light alfs.

5. Svartalfheim: world of the dark alfs.

6. Midgard: the human world.

7. Niflheim: world of ice.

8. Muspelheim: world of fire.

9. Helheim: the underworld.

Each world has different beings, elements, and powers associated with it. Yggrasil is the World-Tree that supports the entire structure. Three good and useful books on Norse cosmology are *Exploring the Northern Tradition* by Galina Krasskova, *Pathwalkers Guide to the Nine Worlds* by Raven Kaldera, and *Essential Asatru* by Diana Paxson. I also recommend *Norse Myths* by Kevin Crossley-Holland, and *Gods and Myths of Northern Europe* by H.R. Ellis Davidson. These will provide a more in-depth study of the cosmology. However, as I stated previously, you should feel free to adapt this exercise to your own cosmology as needed. I'm first and foremost a magician, and we tend to be an extremely pragmatic bunch. Do what works.

Once you've successfully managed to ground in two worlds, try to ground in three—Midgard, Yggdrasil, and Helheim, for example. Make sure each grounding channel is of equal strength and stability, and take some time to experience this and note how different it feels from a single grounding thread. A multifaceted, multi-world ground is something that evolves over time. Every time you make a significant change to your energy body, give yourself time to adjust. Give yourself time—days, weeks, even months—to integrate that change before adding something else.

You can actually ground in any of the nine worlds. An advanced exercise involves extending a two-way ground into the earth and then one to each of the nine worlds, all at the same time.[9] Be aware that you will likely need permission from each of the worlds to do this. It is also possible to ground in Ginungagap, the primal Void, but this is extremely dangerous and should only be attempted after you've mastered nine-worlds grounding, if at all. I know experienced magicians who blanch at the thought, and I've never met a sensible energy-worker who would even entertain the notion. The Void can take from you far more than you can take from it, and it will do so much quicker than you realize. To quote a friend of mine, "Midgard is where you live, the body you live in, the feelings you have, what you think and what you do, how you feel about yourself and your life. It is your subjective reality." Losing one's temporal ground, one's Midgard ground, means that no other ground will be truly stable. Grounding in the Void means grounding in a place so primal that one could easily be sucked in and destroyed unless one's Midgard (temporal, worldly ground) is of equal strength. This can be a surprisingly difficult thing to do when you are balanced against the Void with its almost irresistible pull. There may be times when you may want to ground there temporarily, but you should only do so after extensive experience and only when absolutely necessary.

To recap the advanced exercise:

1. Establish a good Midgard ground in the earth itself. Be a tree.[10]

2. Establish a second channel through which you can draw energy up. Try moving energy into and out of the body in a continual cycle through these two channels.

3. Check your Midgard ground.

4. If that ground is solid, extend another grounding cord into Yggdrasil.

5. Balance out the two grounds, making sure they're of roughly equal strength. It's okay if Midgard is a little stronger.

6. Check both grounds.

7. Extend a third channel into one of the nine worlds.

8. Balance out all three grounds.

9. Create at least two smaller channels or shunts, either into Midgard soil or into the Tree through which you can quickly send incoming energy if you need to.

10. Balance out all of the groundings by drawing energy up and sending it back down to make sure they are all stable and of reasonably equal strength.

11. Once all of this has been done, you can begin to layer on shields and wards.

I would actually do steps one through three and then wait at least a few weeks before continuing on to the next steps. Ideally, establishing this type of ground should be the work of at least a couple of months. It can be very interesting to ground in the ocean or another element, as well. Rooting yourself in a mountain can be a particularly intense grounding experience. However, I've never found anything quite as stable as grounding in the earth—save, perhaps, for extending one's earth ground so far down that it touches the earth's molten core.[11] This can be extremely effective, particularly when you need to rid yourself of unpleasant energies. The fire can purify them. You can also draw energy up from this place.

2

Psi-Gifts

It may seem odd to begin a chapter on psi-gifts by arguing semantics, but that is just what I'm going to do. I believe that precision of language is important, and not making a clear distinction between such things as magic, energy-work, psi-talents, prayer, and religion can lead to sloppy (and from a religious perspective, disrespectful) work.

Psychic ability is a topic of intense interest for many energy-workers, magicians, and Pagans. In fact, some people are first drawn to the various Pagan traditions with the erroneous idea that it is all about magic and virtuosity of the mind. It is true that the spiritual work we do can often serve as a catalyst for rapid growth of psi-talents and lead to a growing awareness of natural energies, but there is a huge difference between magic, psi-talents, and faith. For the Pagans and Heathens reading this book, this is a very important distinction to keep in mind. Psi-talents might enhance the experience of the others, but they're certainly not synonymous.

Perhaps the most prevalent fallacy currently in vogue is the idea of magic or energy-work as religion. It is not. One can have a deep spiritual practice and be very religious and never even think about working magic or engaging in energy-work. Magic is the art of harnessing natural energies through the conduits of psi-gifts and the body to manifest one's will on the material plane. It is the raw manipulation of power.[1] It is the magician and the magician alone who is responsible for the outcome, and that outcome is generally based on focus, will, and skill. Religion, on the other hand, is the worship of Divine forces: Goddesses and Gods. Nor is prayer magic, which is not to say that the two cannot be combined. Energy-workers often use prayer in their work, and I don't think there's anything wrong with that, but it's important to know the difference. Both involve focused intent, but only prayer involves reliance on external forces. To be more specific, when one prays, one does not generally know the outcome; that is in the hands and wisdom of the Deity in question. However, when one casts magic, the outcome may confidently be predicted within a varied set of parameters, which in turn are dependent upon the level and power of the caster. When one does certain types of non-magical energy-work, the results are somewhere in between, depending on what is being done and how. There are times when one may call upon a Deity or when a specific Deity may choose to lend a hand. Admittedly, this can sometimes blur the boundaries between these various practices.

Essentially, though, to worship is to seek communion with the Gods, whereas to act as a magician is to seek to act *as* a god. To act as an energy-worker is to become a bridge, a conduit for power (that is, energy), which may then be directed for specific purposes. This is rarely about shaping the world in accordance with one's will, as it is with magic. Energy-work also tends to be less focused and far more organic. Most energy-workers tread a fine line between purposefully directing energy and relying on some sort of Higher Power to take care of the results. I've found that energy-workers as a whole tend to lack the ruthless focus and arrogance of magicians (as a magician myself, I will admit that we are an incredibly arrogant lot), and I can't say this is a bad thing.[2] One could say that magic (and its related Art of alchemy) is the link between science and religion, and general energy-work is the link between magic and healing. Magic is an act of will and the conscious manipulation of natural energies, whereas basic energy-work is the purposeful involvement of oneself with natural energy, often directing it for specific purposes. That said, magic is a type of energy-work, so at times there can be a very fine line between the two. Much of the difference lies in the attitude and focus of the practitioner. Psi-talents are another thing altogether. Psychic abilities, such as telepathy, empathy, precognition, energy-sight, and the like, are inherent gifts often passed from one generation to another. They are inborn gifts, channels in the matrix of the mind that grant specific perceptive abilities. Of course, it goes without saying that the psychic talents make it that much easier to sense and work with energy.

For now, let's focus on the psi-gifts. I want to make it very clear that these are not in and of themselves magic. There are many variations on these gifts, and each person will experience them somewhat differently. However, the basic gift training remains the same for all of them. There are four important truths to remember:

- These gifts are normal and natural.
- They can be active, latent, or recessive.
- They often run in families, though variations can appear, depending on what gifts run in each parent's line. They are a genetic inheritance, like blue eyes or brown hair.
- They can be developed like a muscle.

An active gift is one that is currently manifesting. You can use it, and it works. A latent gift is one that is not currently active and probably won't be without a great deal of hard work. It might, however, be passed down to one's children. A dormant gift is one that could very easily be triggered into awakening, or one that will naturally awaken with time and growth.

Generally, people will have one strong gift and one or two lesser talents. These talents can often be used together quite nicely. During the course of training, other gifts may open up and develop. A very strong gift will inevitably be passed to one's children to some degree. This is why the same gifts tend to crop up in bloodlines over and over again. Some gifts, such as telepathy and empathy, can be receptive or projective, meaning you may be able to send or receive thoughts or emotions, sometimes both. It's also worth noting that gifted people usually have a unique relationship with others who have the same gift. For some it's very comforting to be around people who are like them. I have found this to be so with empaths, as it adds a whole new dimension to communication. However, for others, especially telepaths, it can be very jarring to be with their own kind.

I like to break the various talents down into the following five categories:

1. Communication talents

Telepathy

Empathy

Animal telepathy

Psychometry

2. Healing talents

Empathy

Physical healing

Mind healing

Land healing

Gift catalysts

3. Talents of physical manifestation

Telekinesis

Pyrokinesis

4. Talents of sight

Precognition

Postcognition

Energy sight

Far sight/remote viewing

5. Miscellaneous Talents

Mediumship

Flukes

Tapping

Generators

Grouping the gifts in such neat categories is actually somewhat problematic, as there is often a great deal of overlap between them. For example, someone with healing may be using a great deal of energy sight, or an empath may receive visual images solely through the emotional resonance. In the case of the empath, is that sight or just empathy? One could make a convincing argument either way. Psychometry is a perfect example of this: I could just as easily have classified it as a gift of seeing, as some psychometrists receive the information visually, but many more will get feelings that are then interpreted, or images paired with feelings. As the saying goes, your mileage may vary.

From my experience as a teacher, the gifts of sight are the most prevalent, followed closely by the gifts of communication. Each gift has certain dangers that must be guarded against. Most commonly this involves becoming severely overwhelmed by the constant stimuli. This will be discussed later on in the section on empathy.

Communication Talents

Telepathy

The gifts of communication typically involve some degree of telepathy. This is generally described as the ability to hear other people's thoughts, especially the surface thoughts. It is most commonly seen in action between family members or close friends. In its lightest form, it can manifest in such ways as answering a question before it's voiced, "plucking" answers to questions you didn't know you knew seemingly out of no-where, and knowing when a family member is thinking about you and wishing you would call. Those with a stronger ability can read the surface thoughts of strangers and, with practice, can learn to probe quite deeply. Even when the gift isn't devel-oped enough to tease out specific individual thoughts, crowds may be uncomfortable for the telepath due to the "white noise" caused by the press of many thoughts and psyches.

This gift can also manifest as an ability to *send* thoughts, which can sometimes enable the telepath to strongly influence another person. Animal telepathy is similar except that the gift is attuned to the frequency of animals rather than that of peo-ple. Generally if a person has one manifestation of the gift, he or she can develop the others.[3]

Much of what is written about empathy can also be said of telepathy, except in the case of telepathy, the stimulus is thought-born rather than emotional. It is very difficult to lie to a gifted telepath; he or she will usually be quite aware of when your words do not match your thoughts and true motivations. Most telepaths are able to strike a comfortable balance between shielding and swimming in the tide of incoming thoughts. It is exhausting to shield every stray thought of every single person all of the time, so telepaths quickly learn how much they can tolerate. Any effort on the telepath's part to probe another psyche deeply affects both psyches and requires a very deft touch. All people, gifted or not, have defenses in their psyches, and the telepath who does this sort of thing needs to be aware of "mind traps." If you visualize the psyche as a landscape or building that can be traversed or explored,[4] a mind trap is like a room with a door that suddenly slams shut, a pool of quicksand from which one must struggle to escape, or even what feels like a physical blow to the mind. There can be a great deal of pain or rage contained in these parts, and entering them can create an onslaught of similar emotions in the telepath who is doing the probing.

Interestingly, telepathy is not language-dependent; the other person's thoughts will translate automatically into the native language of the telepath. I have an acquaintance who is a fairly gifted telepath. He worked for many years in retail and would often interact with people who didn't speak English as part of his job. He had a gift (quite literally!) for figuring out almost immediately what these non-English speakers wanted. His secret, of course (which I knew but his employer didn't), was that he was using telepathy!

Given what I know about empaths, it can be said that emotion tends to be truer than thoughts. To really develop the gift of telepathy, one not only has to accurately read thoughts and the truth of those thoughts, but the attendant emotions as well.

A telepath reads emotions in a far more detached manner than an empath does. For the telepath, emotion is observed rather than directly experienced—rather like reading a book. If you liken thoughts to water, the telepath can gauge how important they are to the psyche being read by feeling them as anything from gentle undulations to the deluge of a tidal wave. Emotions also control the temperature of the water.

Shielding one's telepathic gift is best done by visualizing a wall within one's mind that nothing can breach. The wall can be hard or flexible, depending on the desires of the person building it, but it must be envisioned as insurmountable and impenetrable, completely protecting the mind and the channel for telepathy. An effective visualization for shielding is to picture the gift-channels as actual tubes within the matrix of the mind. All one has to do is shield the channel itself. Of course, this is easier said than done. I will discuss this in more depth in the chapter on shielding and warding.

Empathy

Empathy is the ability to intimately experience, sense, and/or read another person's emotions. It is a strange gift, one that is often misunderstood, and this can be devastating to the person possessing it, as it is the one psychic gift that is intimately connected to one's own emotional state. Empathy is usually defined as the ability to feel another person's emotions, to experience them directly and intimately as though they are one's own. This is not to be confused with sympathy, the ability to relate strongly to someone's feelings. Some theorize that empathy is a weak form of telepathy, but I have found them to be two totally different gifts with totally different resonances and, more importantly, two completely different channels within the matrix of the mind. To an empath, emotions are the primary sense, the means by which he/she experiences the world.

Without proper training, this ability can be somewhat traumatic.[5] If thoughts are accompanied by strong emotions, the empath will be able to read them, but this is not telepathy. This gift usually twins with some degree of healing, though it is considered both a gift of healing and a gift of communication.[6]

A friend of mine once gave me a tongue-in-cheek definition of what it is like to be an empath:

> "You might be an empath if you hate personal contact, have seriously contemplated becoming a hermit and living as far away from people as possible, have ever felt enraged or like crying or laughing a split second after being totally calm and for no apparent reason (and this corresponds to someone new coming into your general vicinity), know upon first meeting a person whether they will be friend [or an] acquaintance or to stay the hell away 'cause they got weird vibes, dude...."

Humorous though this may be, it's not far from wrong.

Empathy can be a very lonely gift. Although empaths experience a rich tapestry of emotions from others, that same gift can effectively cut them off from their own. Physical touch, especially, may feel painful or like a violation. Indeed, it is difficult to shield the gift when there is any physical contact at all, no matter how inconsequential. The empath is exposed to the full spectrum of another person's feelings, feelings that are often overlaid with thoughts and images. This is especially painful when someone's words or actions don't match their emotions or hidden motivations. An empath will feel that lack of cohesion and truthfulness as a physical assault.

This brings up the most difficult problem: It is very easy for an empath, even a well-trained one, to become lost in the flood and turmoil of others' emotions. This can lead to immense psychological disturbance and/or withdrawal from people, and the development of what is called an avoidant personality. One of the most devastating combinations of talents is empathy twinned with an extremely strong gift of mediumship. The resulting stimuli can literally drive a person mad unless he or she has a very strong support group and is given proper training in grounding, centering, and shielding very early on.

Most empaths do not draw nourishment from being among groups of people; instead, they need time alone to recharge, no matter how enjoyable a given group activity may be. If you have this gift, it's important to allow yourself this time.[7] With this gift more than any other, working on establishing and maintaining good boundaries is essential. Psychological and emotional boundaries are important for everyone, but this holds true to an even higher degree for empaths. Do whatever psychological work is necessary; own your issues and deal with them as best you can, understand and acknowledge your own motivations, and accept your "shadow." The ancient maxim "know thyself" is often touted as being extremely important in occult and spiritual work within many different traditions, but it's an absolute necessity for empaths. If you don't know where you end and the other person begins (on every level—emotionally, psychologically, physically, and spiritually), you'll drown in the morass of your own gift.

There are many degrees of empathy, and once an empath starts working magically or with any type of energy, the gift can radically strengthen. It is an incredible healing gift that usually (but not always) indicates the gift of either physical healing or mind healing. In the case of physical healing, the empath is able to accurately sense energy blockages, tension, and pain within the body; with mind healing, he or she is able to sense, read, and/or heal the very fabric of a traumatized or unbalanced mind. Depending on the strength of the gift and the skill of the empath, he or she can even journey directly into a person's inner landscape. Regardless of whether or not they can heal, most empaths are able to soothe raw emotions and occasionally influence the emotional state of others.[8] It is also an invaluable teaching tool. Students should be aware that it is nearly impossible to lie convincingly to an empath, as it is the nature of the gift to be able to see beyond mere platitudes and masks.

The first indication that a person may be an empath is extreme sensitivity to or an unusual awareness of the emotions of others, without the need for verbal or body language cues. Unfortunately, in magical practice, the emphasis is all too often on merely seeing energy rather than feeling it, when both are valid means of harnessing power.[9] Indeed, at its stronger levels, empathy can grant its own type of sight. Regardless of whether one is learning to use the gift for magic or healing, or simply training it as a means of survival, the means of mastering the gift are the same: grounding, centering, and shielding. In fact, these three simple exercises comprise the foundation on which all magic or gift-work is based, regardless of the gift.

Psychometry

Psychometry is the ability to acquire information, read feelings, and occasionally receive images by touching something. It always involves a certain degree of empathy and usually (but not always) some degree of sight, as well. Just as most empaths are shy about touching people because of the nature of their gift, those with psychometry will have the same hesitation about touching objects, because objects absorb and retain the residual energies, especially emotional energies, of those who have held them.

Healing Talents

Mind healing and physical healing

Mind healing and physical healing are fairly self-explanatory. The former is the ability to manipulate the threads of a person's psyche to bring about positive healing, and is almost always empathy-based. A gifted mind healer can actually "rewire" the patterns of a person's psyche. A physical healer, on the other hand, uses natural energy to heal the body. I am not a healer myself, so the best I can suggest here is to gain a thorough understanding of anatomy and physiology. Many with this gift are drawn to alternative healing modalities such as massage, acupuncture, qi gong, and medicinal herbology. The study of any or all of these modalities can only enhance one's awareness of and ability to use this gift. I make no distinction between healing of people and healing of animals because the gift and the means by which it works are the same in both cases.

Land healing

Those with a talent for land healing have a combination of two gifts: a sensitivity to or awareness (through empathy or sight) of the levels of power, currents of energy, and the threads and ley lines that run through the land; and an ability to purposefully manipulate that energy.

Gift catalysts

A gift catalyst (which I consider to be a communication gift as well as a healing gift) consciously or unconsciously uses telepathy, empathy, or mind-healing to open and unlock someone's natural, latent gifts. Gift catalysts tend to be very strong in empathy, healing, or telepathy. They are also the best at identifying gifts, even latent ones, in others.

Talents of Physical Manifestation

Talents of physical manifestation are those that bestow the ability to manifest one's energy very densely on the physical plane and thus impact it directly. There are two gifts that fall into this category: telekinesis (TK) and pyrokinesis (PK). These gifts are rare. When they do manifest, usually unexpectedly, the negative reactions of those around the gifted person may traumatize him or her to the point that he/she refuses to develop or use it again. Fear is rarely a good teacher where psi-gifts are concerned; in fact, it can cause a gift to shut down in a child. In addition, with gifts it's "use it or lose it," so that attitude will shut down the strongest of gifts in time.

Telekinesis

Telekinesis is the ability to move objects with the mind. It often manifests first in adolescence and is responsible for many reports of poltergeist activity. It will often manifest under times of stress or emotional upheaval. Those with this gift learn to purposefully manipulate the electromagnetic fields of things around them. Following are some basic exercises that I was taught to begin training TK:

- Take a set of dice. Focus on a specific number as you throw them and, extending your will into and around the dice, attempt to make them roll that number. Dice are very easy to manipulate this way, even for the completely untrained person.

- Secure a pinwheel in an upright position. Clear your mind, focus on the pinwheel, and "push" with your mind so that it begins to spin. Try not to be attached to the outcome. Often, persistent inability is just a matter of nervousness and performance anxiety.

    ◈ Set a small rubber ball on a flat surface and try to move it with your mind. Then work up to larger objects.

I've also found that being around other psi-talents, particularly those that share your own talent, can be very helpful in developing this and any other gift. Sometimes it's just a matter of being in an environment in which you are seeing clearly that these things are a.) accepted and b.) possible for you to gain the inner confidence necessary to actively manifest your gift.

Pyrokinesis

Pyrokinesis is the ability to control temperature and fire with the mind. Again, this gift seems to manifest most often during times of stress or emotional distress. Therefore, you can see that emotional stability is extremely important for someone with this gift. A colleague of mine once told me that every single person he's known who could actively and consistently manifest this gift was in some way mentally unbalanced. I have not found this to be true, but it is worth considering. My colleague speculated that it had something to do with the fire energy coursing through the neural pathways of the brain. The one person I knew who could consistently do this was somewhat volatile but otherwise perfectly sane and well-grounded (though she did have a terrible temper that she fought to get under control for years). In her, the gift would only manifest when she was extremely angry, which is in itself an unbalanced state. Pyrokinesis can be dangerous to the bearer unless he or she learns early on to channel the excess energy into the earth (that is, to ground). Given how often this gift is tied to emotional extremes, learning to control one's emotions is of utmost importance. Following are a few exercises I learned throughout the years to help develop this gift:

৯৯ Light a candle. Clear your mind and focus on the candle flame. Try to actively affect it by moving it over to one side and the other, making it higher, and then putting it out—all with your mind.

৯৯ Fill a bowl with cold water. Focus on the bowl and on seeing the molecules that make up the water. When something gets hot, it's actually the result of molecules speeding up their motions. The molecular structure becomes agitated and heat is the result. So, focus on the water and heat it up to boiling if you can.

৯৯ Focus on an unlit candle and try to light it with your mind. Work up to larger fires. Always have a fire extinguisher nearby.

Part of the challenge with both of these gifts lies in finding the appropriate channel in your mind matrix and using it properly. Things get much easier once you've achieved your goal once—after this point, your subconscious realizes that it is indeed possible, and this removes a major psychic/psychological block.

No shielding techniques are particularly useful against gifts of this category. If a telekinetic wants to move you, you will move. The only defense is to attack with a strong telepathic or empathic blast, thus destroying their center and keeping them off balance long enough that they can be taken out of commission. Both gifts tend to manifest primarily within the person's line of sight, although with practice this can change, especially if the telekinetic or pyrokinetic also has one of the gifts of sight.

Talents of Sight

The gifts of sight fall into four categories: precognition, postcognition, energy sight, and far sight/remote viewing. Precognition (pre-cog) and postcognition (post-cog) are essentially flip sides of each other.

Precognition

Precognition is the ability to read possibilities and potentialities—the future.[10] It can manifest many different ways, depending on the strength of the gift. Rune-workers and gifted diviners often develop a degree of this, in their ability to read the fluctuation of the Wyrd-web. Essentially precognition has four primary manifestations:

1. Simple intuition: a feeling, a *knowing* that something will occur. If the person is empathic, this feeling can strengthen through contact or as the time of the incident draws closer.

2. The ability to read the threads of Wyrd, seeing all the various possibilities at once and often overlaid upon normal vision.

3. Strong visions of what is to come, usually of incidents that are surrounded by strong emotion.

4. Dreams of future occurrences.

This can be a very disturbing and difficult gift to accept, as what is most often sensed are negative occurrences (because the emotions connected to these events will be the strongest). This gift twins extremely well with empathy, as images are often carried by emotion, and it is actions resulting from emotional motivation that most often affect future possibilities.[11] The important thing to remember is that the future is not set. Seeing something does not make it a foregone conclusion. It is useful and often necessary to learn detachment from the images or visions, watching them flow past like images on a movie screen. With a very strong gift, however, these visions can be total sensory experiences, so this may not always be possible. Lighter versions of this gift most often manifest in very subtle ways, such as knowing exactly who is on the phone before you pick it up. It sounds silly, but it's a viable place to begin. Reading tarot will strengthen this gift, too, as will rune-work. If the gift manifests in dreams, keeping a dream journal is often a useful practice. Some people find the study of Jungian dream analysis helpful, as well. For those who want to sharpen their dream abilities, working with a dream pillow can be somewhat helpful. I recommend the following recipe:

Take a square of dark cloth roughly six inches by six inches. Sew around three sides and affix a zipper to the fourth. Fill this pillow with the following herbs:

- 3 parts mugwort (this herb tends to bring clear, sharply lucid dreams all on its own)
- 1 part chamomile
- 1 part hops
- 1 part chapel flowers doused with jasmine oil (allow to dry thoroughly before adding to the pillow)
- 1 part rose petals doused with rose oil (allow to dry thoroughly before adding to the pillow)
- 1 part vervain
- A small amethyst

Sleep with this pillow near your face. Alternatively, you can use a pouch instead of a pillow and sleep with it near your head.

Sometimes there is very little warning before active precognition kicks in; the dreams, visions, or intense knowledge will come unbidden and unannounced, and there is nothing one can do to stop them. With all the gifts in this category, it's often difficult for the gifted person to gauge how people will react to his or her gift. This can be frustrating for the gifted person. He or she has to come to terms with other people's reactions to their gift, which can range from belief to complete denial. For people who are particularly gifted, the strength of their visions has nothing to do with the level of intimacy they have with the people involved. As with all the gifts, it is important to realize that this is not mental illness. It's a very natural manifestation of an innate talent, just like a gift for mathematics or musical virtuosity. There are also people in the world who are so open to the idea of precognition that gifted people tend to see an unusual amount of future occurrences in their presence. These people are Wyrd-channels, "transistors" for the energy of those shifting potentialities and possibilities. If a gifted person has a strong degree of projective empathy or telepathy, he/she may be able to project images into the mind/consciousness of another person. This is very rare, but it's a useful defensive talent in a gift that is usually not. Especially in the matter of the death of a loved one, being able to see the future could change the gifted person's reaction to the death when and if it occurs. He or she would start the grieving process at the point of the seeing rather than the actual death.

Postcognition

Postcognition is precognition in reverse. With this gift, one may receive images of the past and be able to read the past deeds of others, especially via objects or certain locales. This can manifest in the exactly same way as precognition. It also twins very well with empathy. Again, the consciousness will be drawn to incidents that are accompanied by extreme emotion, which leaves a psychic imprint. Someone with both post-cog and empathy would be very good at psychokinesis (reading the past from objects which hold resonance of the owner).[12]

Remote viewing

Remote viewing (which my teacher called "far sight") is the ability to see events in real time that are occurring far away from the viewer. Again, the sight may be drawn to emotions but this is not always so. Astral projection is very easy for those with even a hint of this gift, as is lucid dreaming.

I'm in no way a seer, but here are a few exercises I've picked up over the years that may prove useful to those who are:

- Take a deck of cards. Remove each card face down from the deck and run your hands over it. Go through the deck and try to determine the color of each one. When you reach 100-percent accuracy, do it again for suit. When you're accurate at that, try to guess what each card is—suit, number, and court. If you have a partner to practice with, have your partner look at each card, and then write down what it is without your partner telling you. (It should be noted that neither of these exercises is pure sight; the first incorporates a touch of psychometry, and the latter, a touch of telepathy.)

- Learn to read tarot. This is an excellent way to train and develop precognition. The cards are merely visual devices that allow you to "key" your consciousness into your pre-cog. It's a way of circumventing your internal censors.

- Keep a dream journal. This tends to be useful for seers who tend toward a facility for dreaming.

There are a number of books out there on how to project astrally. I have done this myself a number of times, and found it unpleasant and nauseating. That said, I was taught two exercises to develop this facility, so I pass them on here.

Go on a liquid fast for a week. It sounds odd, but the idea is to weaken the physical body's hold on the astral body. There is a skill to fasting. One should not simply begin a fast or break a fast. One should take as many days to go into a fast as one will actually be fasting. The same goes for breaking a fast. If you plan to fast for five days, then take five days to ease into it, decreasing your food intake little by little, and then take five days to bring yourself back up to solid food. (For the love of the Gods do not break a fast by having a full meal—you'll seriously regret it!) No matter what, you should always consult a healthcare professional before going on a fast, particularly if you have health issues, are on medication, or have any blood-sugar issues. If you are unable to do a full fast, you can do a modified fast with less discomfort and achieve almost the same results. Cut all animal protein, all sugar, and all processed foods out of your diet for a specified amount of time. Keep in mind that this can cause mood changes.

During your fast, practice the following breathing pattern twice day for 15 minutes: block your left nostril and inhale for four counts through your right nostril; block both nostrils and hold your breath for 16 counts; block the right nostril, unblock the left, and exhale through the left for eight counts. Then do it in reverse. As you practice this exercise, you want to slowly but steadily increase your count, always following the same pattern (4-16-8, 8-32-16, 16-64-32, and so on). Each day, do three sets of 20 repetitions in each sitting. A repetition is a full round as described above.

Energy sight

Energy sight is perhaps one of the most common forms of sight. It is the ability to see energy, auras, elementals, non-corporeal beings, Vaettir, and manifestations of Deity. It's an excellent gift for a magician to have. It's also very useful for healers, as most healers need to be able to see the energy blockages of their patients. This gift often twins with mediumship. If someone with energy sight has another gift, their sight will influence their perceptions of the energy resonances of that gift—for example, if they are empaths, they won't only feel the emotions, but they will also see that emotional energy in some form. The same goes for telepaths. Most people have a touch of energy sight; however, a strong gift in another category may overpower it such that it may become difficult to recognize.

Miscellaneous Talents

Mediumship

Mediumship is the ability to hear, see, feel, smell, and interact with non-corporeal beings. The gift most often twins with energy sight. It is the most seductively dangerous of the gifts, as mediums naturally lack a strong grip on the physical world. They are so loosely anchored in their physical bodies that it is very easy for non-corporeal entities to come in and take over. It's not that they lack willpower; rather, their astral bodies simply aren't particularly well-grounded. For this reason, extra attention must be paid to the basic exercises. Even then, grounding will always be a struggle for them. Indeed, many mediums don't want to ground, even if they aren't consciously aware of this resistance. The dead are often more real to them than the living, and many mediums have far deeper and closer relationships with the dead than they do with the living. Grounding and shielding puts up a boundary that can make mediums feel as though they are being cut off from their closest friends. It's a problematic gift to have.[13]

It is important for active mediums to realize that spirits and other non-corporeal entities can be as annoyingly ignorant as humans. Death does not confer great wisdom. Don't always take what a spirit says as truth; they can be deceitful, so be careful. Most mediums, if they're lucky, develop a very strong relationship with at least one or two positive spirits. They talk to them often and trust has been established on both sides. These mediums usually practice the development of their gift with those particular spirits. I generally suggest working with one's ancestors to develop this gift. I also suggest learning how to carefully ward a room, and doing it before calling on one's spirits (something that we'll discuss in a later chapter).

Opening oneself up to any spirit is always a risky venture and the budding medium should try to have others present, especially those with sight who have experience, when developing this gift. A good rule of thumb is don't call anything you can't banish. If it has glowing red eyes, it's bad. If there is a stench, it's bad. If it seems all-knowing, it's bad. If what it's telling you seems too good to be true or is just what you want to hear, it's bad. Most beneficent spirits will make an effort to change their appearance when they are told that their present incarnation is disturbing. Spirits will often be attracted to mediums because they have a desire and a need to communicate. This is especially true of ghosts. This can be draining for the medium, so it's perfectly okay to tell the spirit(s) to come back later. As I once told a distraught medium, "Just because they're dead doesn't mean you have to talk to them."

One of the most profound experiences—and duties—of a medium is to aid the soul in its passage to the other side. Often mediums will find themselves strongly called by Deities of the underworld for just this purpose. It is important for those without the gift to not put undue pressure on mediums to explain away all the mysteries of death just because they can see spirits. And it is important for mediums to resolve their own issues with death. Depending on the strength of the gift, natural and unnatural disasters can affect a medium greatly, as can locations where disasters or tragedies have occurred.[14]

In some religious practices, believers are trained to work within a specific system of experiencing these non-corporeal beings. Mediums should learn to recognize these systems and regard them as sacred. An example would be Santeria. (However, I would suggest asking permission first before chatting with their ancestors.) Respect and courtesy dictate that the medium should honor the various hierarchies inherent in these systems.

Mediumship can prepare one for Divine possession but it is generally not a good idea to invite anything other than Deity to come in and take up residence. I actually find that mediums make very poor vessels for Divine possession. For some reason, despite the fact that they seem the same, the two talents are actually quite different; in fact, they are often mutually exclusive, though I've no idea why. Additionally, not all mediums are able to see spirits; some hear them instead. This is called clairaudience.

I've worked with enough shamans, God-servants, and spirit-workers to know that sometimes, when a Deity feels it is necessary, He/She will temporarily give someone the ability to experience a gift that the person doesn't normally have. For example, if you don't possess the gift of mediumship but are the only possible source of aid available to help a spirit, if you ask Deity you will be shown quite clearly what to do. This can occasionally leave a person with a newly opened gift-channel.

The best way to learn to cope with the gift of mediumship is to a.) ground and center *ad nauseum et ad infinitum*, and b.) develop a relationship with your ancestors. Ancestors include deceased relatives as well as those who were close enough to be kin or spiritual kin. Talk to them. Set up an ancestral altar with images, food offerings, candles, incense, glasses of fresh water—anything that piques your interest and or sets off your intuition. Make your own ancestors a part of your life. They can provide help and, more importantly, protection. Ask them for this protection. It is important. If you are adopted, you have two sets of ancestors you can call upon. Non-relatives who occupy a powerful place in your life, such as guides, teachers, mentors, or friends, may be honored, as well. Continue the relationship through the reciprocity of offering and honoring.

Flukes

Everyone with a psi-gift occasionally runs into a fluke. Flukes are people who may or may not have a gift of their own, but who are naturally resistant to the influence of the gifts of others. For this reason it can be very difficult for gifted people to be around them. Although they are not purposefully shielding, they are almost totally unreadable. Sometimes they are extremely gifted people who have developed iron-clad shields as a survival mechanism.[15] Gifts simply will not work in the presence of one of these people. Flukes are also usually very disturbed by sensitives.

Tapping

Tapping is an extraordinarily rare gift. In all my years of teaching, I've only run into it twice. Someone with this gift is able to link energy with another person, thereby allowing that person to temporarily commandeer the tapper's own psi-gift(s) and/or augment his or her own gift(s). I've also seen it used to temporarily grant a physical sense to someone who lacked it. In the case I witnessed, the tapper linked energy with someone who had no sense of smell and, for a brief time, allowed that person to use her own sense of smell. It was fascinating to witness. I believe that tapping is related to being a catalyst, though it may be pure coincidence that the two people I knew who possessed tapping were also gift catalysts.

Generators

This is another rare gift. Some people are born with the ability to amp up other gifts or channel a great deal of energy into a working. It's as if they're psychic and energetic generators. They are often lacking in the other psi-talents (except for sight), and often have a great deal of difficulty grounding, centering, and really staying focused in the mundane world. Occasionally they have the gift of mediumship. The problem with generators is that, like mediums, they're not particularly well-connected to their physical bodies or the physical world. They also tend to be rather flighty and they usually don't have the strongest wills. Common sense is not their strong suit. They also tend to attract a great deal of unwelcome and occasionally dangerous attention, for the precise reason that this gift is so rare and its bearers so pliable.

If you happen to be a generator, ground as though your life depended on it. Work hard to develop regular habits of centering, grounding, and shielding. If you can afford it, study a martial art. It will help develop exquisite body awareness, is very grounding, and can provide some much-needed discipline. Better yet, do as little occult or energy-work as possible. This is not a gift that needs to be developed. If you are very lucky, you might find an ethical teacher or magician who is willing to provide protection, but this can be a dangerous proposition for both sides. I have seen this kind of protection negotiated in exchange for the magician having access to the generator's gift to augment the power of the magician's workings. This means that the "protector" has to be vigilant to keep the proverbial wolves from trying to steal or harm the generator, and the generator is rendered completely dependent on someone else for that protection. All in all it's a headache regardless of how it's managed. It's not a good situation either way, though it is an option. I certainly wouldn't do it, though.

Magic

Magic is the harnessing and manipulation of natural energies, which are then directed through the conduit of the body in accordance with the will. The practice of magic is not a psi-gift per se, though people with strong psi-gifts are more open to developing this skill. Psi-gifts enhance the experience of and ability to work magic. What clouds the issue slightly is that there is a specific psi-gift, a very specific mind-channel, that enables one to sense, internalize, and actively manipulate high levels of energy. I call it the "magician's gift," as it enables the energy-worker or magician to develop a level of skill that far exceeds what those who lack this gift could ever attain. It also enables the magician to tap into higher levels of power without the risk of harm that an ordinary energy-worker would incur. Not everyone has this channel, just as not everyone has the requisite channel for sight or empathy.

Psychic Vampires

A psychic vampire is a person genetically wired to require *prana*, or life energy, the way that traditional vampires require blood. There is evidence that this talent is genetic, as it tends to run in families just as the other psychic gifts do. There are two basic types of psychic vampires: primary vampires, who are born that way; and secondary vampires, who either learn the skill as a survival mechanism somewhere along the way or who are purposefully modified via energy-work. The best book out there on this particular talent, which is somewhat beyond the scope of this volume, is *The Ethical Psychic Vampire* by Raven Kaldera.

Psychic vampirism can be an extremely useful gift. A skilled psi-vamp can suck pain, depression, anger, and sorrow out of people, gaining sustenance from the negative emotions while helping the person they "feed" upon. They can also "digest" very negative, tainted, or unpleasant energies in locales and objects, thus cleansing these things very effectively. There are drawbacks to having this particular talent, though, and certain caveats a psi-vamp needs to be aware of. For any readers who suspect that they might be or know a psi-vamp, I highly recommend Kaldera's book.

The various gifts can combine in surprising ways. The thing to remember is not to be afraid of experimenting and actively using your talents. Practice centering, grounding, and shielding (the subject of our next chapter), and try to enjoy the process of developing these inborn talents.

3

Shielding

After centering and grounding, the next important technique to learn is shielding. Many people tend to use the terms "shielding" and "warding" interchangeably; indeed, I myself have been guilty of this on occasion. However, a ward is a protection placed on a place or thing, whereas a shield is a protection placed on a person—at least, that is what I was taught.

Shields are necessary. We lock our doors when we go outside. We wear warm clothing in winter. We put on sunscreen at the beach. Shielding one's aura is exactly the same thing: good psychic common sense. It prevents a plethora of problems. I have encountered several people (usually it's an energy-worker) who are very resistant to the idea of shielding. They want to be one with the universe, even when that oneness is driving them crazy. Somehow, they have come to equate shielding with walling themselves off from humanity. Nothing could be further from the truth. A shield is a flexible filter that one can adapt to suit one's needs and circumstances. It is a boundary, and boundaries are good things. They are necessary things. They make us more efficient (and sane—let's not forget about sane). They tell us where we begin and where the incoming stimulus ends.

Again, you don't have to be especially psychic to do these exercises; they are for everyone. In fact, most psychics I know would be painfully glad if *everyone* learned them! Walking around unshielded is similar to walking naked, with your wallet and valuables in hand, into a room full of thieves. To someone who is psi-talented, it can feel as though you are walking into a room screaming at full volume and wielding a sledgehammer. Learning to shield is a matter not only of common sense but also of simple psychic courtesy. For those who feel ambivalent about the entire concept of shielding, perhaps it will help to think of it not as shielding others out, but of shielding oneself in. After all, knowing where we begin and end, where our energy and emotions begin and end, what is us and what is coming in from the outside, is essential to authentic, effective communication.

We're going to begin by discussing personal shields. These are shields that one raises to guard against outside influence or attack. They make the world bearable and prevent overstimulation of the senses and the sickness that can come along with that. They are absolutely essential for those with certain talents, especially empathy and telepathy. They're useful for people with minimal gifts, as well. They keep our emotions and thoughts from leaking, which in turn will help us better maintain our emotional equilibrium. Good shielding keeps us from being influenced by the needs, desires, and emotions of those around us—unless, of course, we choose to be so influenced. It also keeps us from internalizing other people's tension and stress. Remember when I said that it's very important to know where you begin and end on every possible level? Well, shielding makes that possible. Centering and grounding comprise the foundation upon which a shield must rest. Basically, think of your shield as an energetic hazmat suit.

As you may be able to see from this brief description, there are two necessary types of shields: psychic shields and energetic shields.[1] Psychic shields are constructed within the mind to shield specific gifts, whereas energetic shields are constructed to shield against external energies and, if necessary, magical attack. Psychic shields protect on a psychic level—for example, they make it far more comfortable for an empath or telepath to be around you. Energetic shields, on the other hand, protect on a magical and energetic level. They prevent unwanted energy from attaching to your aura or entering the sphere of your astral/etheric body and doing harm. Ideally, you should develop both types of shields independently from each other. A psychic shield is not enough to protect against magical attack or energetic contamination, nor is an energetic shield always enough to prevent psi-attack or overstimulation. With just a little practice and concentration, even someone who lacks skill or talent can learn to maintain both types of working shields.

Shielding can be a very complex process. At advanced levels, someone can have various layers of interlocking shields supporting and complementing each other. The idea (particularly with energetic shields) is to construct a layered matrix that can withstand repeated battering without ever collapsing and which cannot easily be breached. There is a caveat with all this shielding, however: the more complex the shield matrix, the easier it is for someone with a strong psi-gift or magic to tell that you know what you're doing. In many cases it advertises that you're someone with a strong gift and that you know how to use it. As this isn't always desirable, it's useful to learn how to camouflage your shields. This is something that we'll be discussing in more detail a little later on in the chapter.

Both types of shields have their benefits and drawbacks. It's important to point out that many people are unable to adequately protect their gift(s). Conversely, those who lack a particular gift are not always able to effectively protect themselves *from* that gift. Sight falls into the first category, and telekinesis, the latter. Psychic shields, or psi-shields, are most important for empaths and telepaths, both of whom may find it very difficult to function socially without them. Mediums require a combination of heavily grounded mental and energetic shielding. And because emotions are energy, empaths require both psychic and energetic shields, as well.

There are two ways that I have learned to shield empathy or telepathy. The most common type of psychic shield involves imagining a wall in your head and then "constructing" it through intense concentration. This wall blocks or filters incoming thoughts and emotions, and can be as flexible or as hard as you wish. Although creating and maintaining one takes constant attention at first, in time it becomes second nature. A skilled telepath or empath can create complex and layered psychic shields that filter, protect, and misdirect. I once encountered a young empath who had the equivalent of a labyrinth protecting that particular gift-channel. He was still able to read with exceptional accuracy, but this labyrinth of psychic shields—almost an inner landscape—provided him the necessary detachment to avoid feeling overwhelmed by his not insubstantial gift.

A problem with this type of shielding—for empaths, at least—is that no matter how great the shielding, it is nearly impossible to shield against physical touch. In fact, I have seen empaths touch a person lightly to verify the honesty or accuracy of a statement. Nothing is more uncomfortable for an empath than detecting a disconnect between someone's internal motivations and external behavior. Most empaths, if they realize what they have, are extremely self-aware where their emotions are concerned. While most people are hardly aware of or able to admit what they're feeling at any given time, the average empath is *always* exquisitely aware of his or her emotional state—and usually everyone else's in his or her general vicinity, as well—and can tease out individual threads and shades of meaning from what most people would identify as a single emotion. The empath can read subtleties. When an empath converses with another empath, simple touch can provide a conduit for images or feelings, thus adding another powerful layer to the means by which they communicate.

Another problem with this type of shielding is that empaths may misread a shield as irritation, annoyance, or even dislike. I know that I myself sometimes read someone's exhaustion or illness as active irritation.[2] This is why clear communication is essential.

A simpler method of shielding, but one that can feel very disconcerting to the person being shielded, is to purposefully "plug" the gift-channel. To this end, I have found it very helpful to conceive of the gift-channels as tubes or pipelines running through the matrix of the mind. One essentially puts a cover on the "pipe" that corresponds to the particular gift. This takes almost no energy, and when done properly it will effectively block a gift almost completely. I do not recommend keeping this type of shield up for more than a few hours, or a day at the most. It is, however, extremely effective.[3]

It's important to raise and maintain your shields before you leave your house. If you are unshielded or your shields are weak, and then you enter an emotionally heated situation or even just a large group of people, the sudden swelling press of emotion can be overwhelming and painful. Once external stimuli get through your shields, it is almost impossible to shield them out again without completely removing yourself from the situation that caused the breach. In such a situation, it's possible for a more experienced energy-worker, magician, telepath, or empath to extend shields over someone who is having shielding trouble, but it's best to avoid this is at all possible. Although energetic shields can't replace good psychic shields, in such a circumstance they're better than nothing because they will disrupt to some degree incoming energies (emotion is, after all, energy). Because empaths are also often quite sensitive to natural energy, I recommend raising an energetic shield in addition to the psychic shield.

Energetic shielding is a bit more complex. Psychic shields will only protect against thoughts and emotions, or empathic or telepathic probes or attacks. They will not in any way protect against magical attack or energetic contamination. Conversely, energetic shields will offer limited protection mentally but excellent protection against magical attack and/or energetic contamination.

In order to shield, it is absolutely necessary to be strongly and deeply centered and grounded first. Without a solid center and ground, it is impossible to maintain a strong and stable shield matrix. You can't build a house without a foundation. Ideally, maintaining an effective shield matrix should be second nature. It's possible to set shields so that they are self-feeding and more or less self-maintaining, save for the inevitable cleaning and repairs should they ever come under attack. The more energy-sensitive one is, the easier it is to tailor shields to one's personal specification (as opposed to simply having a bubble-like force-field, which is what people usually envision at first).

So what happens after you've correctly grounded and centered? Once you've established as strong a ground as possible, choose a power source. What this will be depends on the type of shield you want to construct. Most people are taught to first draw energy from the earth, from the core, or from one of the many lines of power that crisscross beneath the surface. These are called *ley lines*, and the place where multiple lines meet is called a *node*. Levels of these meridians exist almost everywhere; when they are absent, it is usually a sign that the land is unhealthy.

Here's how to shield:

- Center and ground.
- Find a power source.
- Draw energy up and around you.
- Shape the energy to your will and need, making sure it has a power source upon which to feed.
- Make it as permeable or as impermeable as you wish.

(Note: Make sure it doesn't conflict with any other shields you may have. You want each layer of your shield matrix to integrate cleanly. In other words, they need to get along.)

Project onto it a sample of what you want it to do. Think of this as the equivalent of giving a bloodhound the scent of its prey. Tell the shield strongly that *this* is what it should watch for, devour, or deflect. Check it occasionally to make sure it is strong and stable and that it hasn't suffered any tears or damage.

Or, a more simplified version:

๏ Build it.

๏ Feed it.

๏ Tell it what to do.

๏ Perform maintenance as necessary.

Let's use ley lines as an example. Once you are properly centered and grounded, extend your senses into the earth, reaching down with a tendril of consciousness, something akin to an invisible hand, until you touch a ley line. You will feel a little jolt of power, a sense of a key fitting into a lock that tells you you've reached a ley line. Draw energy up carefully, allowing it to flow around you and shape itself to your aura. Make sure it forms a complete sphere. The top and bottom both need to be shielded, too; in fact, I also like to allow a shield to mold itself to my grounding channel. A skilled magician can strike at a person's ground and overload it, if it's not shielded. This is unpleasant. If you can't sense it, "fake it 'til you make it" is the order of the day. Remember, energy follows thought and thought follows imagination, and all of this needs to be disciplined to the will.

The first shields that are usually taught to people are either bubble shields or mirror shields. Both are effective, but both have their drawbacks.

Bubble Shields

This is a very easy, very basic shield to make and maintain. It can be fairly viscous, or permeable enough to filter energy as through a delicate net. Unlike many other shield types, it is fairly comfortable for non-psi people to be around, even when it is not camouflaged. (People can sometimes sense a shield and respond negatively to it. We'll be discussing this more fully in the section on camouflaging shields.) This is a nice shield for an empath to maintain on a regular basis in addition to his or her psychic shields. A bubble shield won't block telepathy, though.

To construct a bubble shield, use the part of your grounding channel that allows you to draw energy up into you. Draw up the necessary energy and bring it up and around you in the form of a bubble (think of an egg or something that completely encompasses you). Or, bring the energy into your body and feel it expanding outward from your solar plexus until it completely encompasses you. Ideally, you want the shield to feel bouncy, as though anything thrown at it would bounce off. If you want to get a little creative, visualize the energy as a soothing color. Doing this can affect the way people respond to your shield. Particularly if it's drawn from earth, I usually see the energy as a golden color. Although this is a nice, comfortable, easy shield to make and maintain, it has absolutely no combat applications whatsoever. It will not hold up to any type of serious attack.

Mirror Shields

As their name indicates, mirror shields are hard shields created to deflect and reflect incoming attack. The external surface of the shield is usually envisioned as diamond-hard and mirror-like.

The best way to construct a mirror shield is to draw energy up around you. As this is a harder, sharper, and more difficult shield to manipulate, I don't recommend bringing energy into you. Shape the energy into a shield, making sure that it sits close to your aura (you don't need a huge, bold shield). Once you create your sphere, focus on the external surface. See and feel it becoming diamond-hard and reflective. I usually envision this shield as either a hard, silver-colored metal, or diamond-like and clear.

I've occasionally slapped a mirror shield on students who couldn't control their gifts, except in these cases I created the shield with the mirror on the *inside* so that everything they inadvertently projected was reflected immediately right back in their faces. This is not a nice thing to do, and only the teacher-student contract we'd entered into gave me the lawful right to do so.

Two caveats: If this shield is constructed properly, incoming attacks will simply bounce off. However, just like a bullet ricocheting in a closed space, what bounces off can strike someone innocent. If this happens, you're karmically responsible for that harm. Also, although this shield's surface is diamond-hard, even diamonds can be shattered if they're struck in the right place and with sufficient force.

Elemental Shields

These are particularly powerful shields that are good for layering. Elemental shields are rarely static, as mirror shields are, and this makes them incredibly flexible and strong. Additionally, if they are crafted correctly, they partake of the essence and power of the element they're drawn from. This is one of those shielding techniques in which the line between magic and energy-work is very grey.

In magic, the four classical elements are Wind, Fire, Water (or Ice), and Earth. A shield crafted from an element will reflect the nature of that element. When you construct these shields, you must remember to work within the boundaries of the element's nature. These forces will always act in accordance to their nature. It helps if you have some hands-on training with the four elements. Some direct understanding of their very real power will help you connect more strongly to their magical essence.

Wind shields

Imagine a tornado or a raging hurricane wind. This is the power you want to infuse your shield with. When you call the energy up around you, you want to purposefully imbue it with the nature of wind. Wind has its ley lines and currents, even nodes, just as the land does ("as above, so below," after all). If necessary, you can tap into this to achieve the necessary pattern. It's not a good idea to tie a shield to these nodes, though. The energies of Wind are very different from the energies of Earth, and they will not tolerate such a binding. If it sounds as though I am intimating that the elements are alive, I am. The elements have consciousness and sentience, though it's very different from human sentience. This consciousness must be respected when drawing on their energies and natures.

So, draw the energy up around you and pattern it to wind energy. Make it feel the way wind feels by achieving the same frequency of energy. If you have permission from the winds to snatch a wisp of true wind to add to and power the shield, then by all means do so. See and feel the energy whirling around you. A good wind shield should have at least two layers that move in different directions. Wind is incredibly powerful. It can destroy cities and wear away stone. In the same way, a well-constructed and well-maintained wind shield can disperse or wear away incoming, hostile energies.

You will note that I continually emphasize maintenance when speaking of shields. There is a reason for this: even the best shields are subject to the contingencies of regular maintenance to stay clean and strong and solid. For beginners, this may mean checking them every hour, or even twice an hour. For more experienced practitioners, it may mean checking them once a month. However you choose to do it, don't just set a shield and forget about it. Look in on it and check it for energy leaks or holes. Do what you need to in order to keep it in good working order. This is your external security system, after all.

Fire shields

Fire shields are cast in much the same way as wind shields, save that you are drawing on the essence of Fire. Feel and see the flame enveloping you. Your aura is the wick in the midst of the candle flame, and the fire is the shield around your aura. The incoming emotions of others, and any hostile energies, form the "oxygen" on which the fire feeds.

This is an easy shield to maintain, and a good candidate to build combat shields around. Fire is particularly useful in combat: it will just eat up whatever is thrown at it. However, it can go into overload if too much is thrown at it at once, which is, of course, a drawback, as it would be with any shield. Part of the essential nature of Fire is that it cleanses and hallows. That is why some religious traditions, such as Heathenry, will often hallow and consecrate a space by carrying fire around its perimeter.

This is also a fairly comfortable shield for others to be around. It is, predictably, warm and inviting. It can also look like part of your aura, which makes it relatively easy to cam-ouflage. It will not make you inconspicuous, though; in fact, people might be drawn to you. Fire shields are good shields for performers to use for just this reason. Of course, you can cloak yourself in a fire storm if you wish, particularly if you are engaged in active combat. This is not something I'd suggest doing on a daily basis, though. When you need to strengthen a fire shield, do so by making the flames hotter and higher.

If you have a good working relationship with Fire, you may be able to tie this shield into Muspelheim, the world of Fire, or some other fire source. Do not—I repeat, *do not*—do this without first obtaining the requisite permissions. For information on world traveling, I suggest Raven Kaldera's book *Pathwalkers' Guide to the Nine Worlds*.

Water shields

Drawing on the power of the ocean, the tidal wave, and the flood, water shields are impressive and exceptionally powerful. There is no place water cannot go, which makes it an incredibly difficult shield to breach. Like wind and fire shields, this is an active, dynamic shield. These elements are made of molecules moving in fluid states. There is nothing static about them.

To make a water shield, draw the water energy up with the roaring force of an ocean wave. Layer this shield by letting one layer wash over you, moving in a circular motion around your auric body from one direction, and then raising a second shield to do the same but from another direction. The perpetual motion of the water comprises the shield. If you have a good working relationship with Water, you may be able to tie this into an actual body of water, but this is a very individual choice. This shield usually feels cool and cleansing to the person casting it. However, if that person has no affinity whatsoever with Water, it can make him or her feel a little nauseous.

Ice shields

Not everyone can work with Ice. I happen to like the feel of this shield, but it can feel cold and remote to those outside its protection. I learned about this shield from a member of Clan Tashlin, though I cast it a bit differently based on my own magical background.

First, I draw upon the energies of the Norse world of Ice, Niflheim. From there I draw a shield of energy around myself. This is very much like a bubble shield, save that it is drawn from Ice energy. I inform the shield that all incoming energy is heat, and the ice will then simply suck the warmth from this energy. Ice that is cold enough to sustain itself will freeze anything it comes into contact with. In this way, the shield devours all incoming energy.

I would suggest having permission to draw from Niflheim. If you work in a different cosmology, however, it's not necessary. You can set an Ice shield by drawing on the nature of Ice, and by setting the shield frequency to feel like ice.

Earth shields

The first earth shield I will teach here I call the "sandstorm." Just as with the wind and water shields, this shield raises a swirling cone of energy around the auric body. In this case, that energy is constructed of earth energy—specifically, that of a sandstorm. This is a very corrosive shield that will break down and disperse all incoming energy. I do not suggest having this shield next to your skin, as it can feel rather abrasive.

For those who prefer shields that don't move, or for beginners who may have trouble with moving shields, it is possible to draw upon the energies of earth to create what I call the "mountain wall." This shield is a wall, as thick and solid as a mountain all around you. Anything that strikes it is stopped by the dense body of earth, just as a bullet fired into the side of a mountain is enveloped and ultimately stopped by the mountain itself. That is the idea here. Some people build this shield brick by brick as they would a wall, while others simply feel the mountain rising around them. The one drawback is that this is a heavy shield that can be difficult to maintain.

Spinning vortex shields

This shield has many pros and cons. It's excellent in combat, but because of this, it's definitely a high-profile shield. The benefit of this shield is that it doesn't require any elemental affinity. Its power comes from the utilization of pure force. It's also very flexible and can be very easily combined with a fire, tornado, sandstorm, or waterspout shield. A major drawback is that it takes concentration and a great deal of energy to maintain. This is not an everyday shield. Like the wind shield, it's constantly in motion, spinning like a tornado around you. It works by dispersing energy or deflecting it forcefully. This shield is cast by drawing up energy from your ground. If you have a strong Air affinity, you can also pull energy right out of the air. That energy becomes a spinning vortex of raw force around your aura.

Under-the-skin shields

In addition to external shields, there are ways of creating protections on or beneath the skin. I would not rely solely on this type of protection, but it can certainly be included as the "backup protection" of a well-constructed matrix of combat shields. It can also be the last line of defense against magical attacks that include leech spells (magical projectiles designed to suck out one's life energy) and elfshot (a magically constructed weapon that will poison the blood and corrode the joints).

To cast this shield, draw energy up from the source of your choice (the grounding channel is good for this). Feel it filling your body, running like liquid just under the skin. Charge this energy in whatever way is most comfortable for you—perhaps to resemble thin, flexible Kevlar or a simple thin bubble—whatever you feel you can live with. Keep it simple. You can also create this type of shield by drawing energy up through your ground, bringing it up through your center and through each chakra until it reaches the crown. Exhale and send the energy out through the crown so that it rains down over your skin. Concentrate on getting a continuous, even flow, allowing the energy to run over your skin or as close to your skin as possible. Envision it absorbing into and remaining right under your skin, or see it adhering, paper-thin, on the surface of the skin. Then charge it to be a densely packed, crackling energy field that will neutralize incoming energy. I recommend setting this particular shield to remain latent until something hits your outer shield, at which point it can become active and "awake." This is done by mentally investing the energy with this knowledge, and commanding it as it is being cast.

It is also possible to create an emergency shield by changing the nature of your aura. I don't recommend this for daily use because it requires a tremendous amount of energy, but if you come under attack, you can actually harden your aura so that it repels incoming energy. This won't hold but a few seconds or so; still, it's a useful emergency skill to have. Another useful trick is to make the aura so viscous that it traps incoming energy and then sheds it as a snake sheds its skin. This can be uncomfortable, but the aura will replenish itself.

Force-field/disrupting shields

This is a very useful shield to add to a layered matrix. It is not strong enough in and of itself to stand as a single shield, but added to a series of layers, it is extremely effective. The energy of electricity or lightening, or even energy from the Void—anything that has an electrical charge to it—can all work well for this. (Use energy from the Void only if you are an experienced magician. It can kill you otherwise.) This is a very thin, very light shield that will disrupt the frequency of any incoming energy, thus dispersing its power. I personally like to use this as my second layer of shields, right beneath my concealment shield, which is the most external layer. It can be cast to resemble a thin net.

Basic auric shield

This is a classic shielding technique that every magician, energy-worker, and psi-talented person should be familiar with. It's based on the Pillar of Light exercise given by Denning and Phillip in their book, *The Art of Psychic Self Defense*, but you will find variations cropping up throughout the occult community. It teaches you to construct a basic personal shield. It's based on work that was being done in occult circles during the early part of the 20th century. It is a particularly good example of the difference between ceremonial magic, which focuses on working the upper crown and third eye chakras and connecting to the aether, and Northern Tradition shamanic work, organic earth magics, and the type of psi-focused magic that I was later taught—all of which place particular emphasis on grounding into the earth.

Begin the following exercise by running through your basic grounding and centering exercises. Once you have both grounded and centered, visualize and feel a glowing sphere of steel-blue light spinning above your crown. It is cosmic force, creative/destructive primal energy, Divine essence. Allow that shower of steel-blue energy to flow down around you. Let it wash over your aura and completely seal you in a protective sphere of power. Regardless of what color your aura is, or what you imagine it to be, this shields it within a force field of steel-blue energy. This force field should extend three or four feet above and below you and at least two feet away from you.

Once you have this field securely set, visualize the interior being flooded with protective white light, light that washes away any stagnant or inhospitable energy. Continue feeling and visualizing this for at least five minutes. Finally, visualize a personal symbol of power—a pentacle, a cross, a valknot, a hammer, whatever—radiating from the force field near your solar plexus. This seals and locks the shield into place. Then go ahead and let it fade from consciousness—it will still be there (though I do recommend doing this exercise several times a day). Once you have mastered this technique, you can begin to experiment and adapt this shield to your needs and preferences. As always, you must be adequately centered and grounded to shield effectively.

Shields are many-faceted. They can be latent, set to activate only when incoming threat is detected; they can be active, always up and ready; or they can be tricky, and include traps to capture and drain energy or tag the sender. They can be purely defensive, or they can include offensive weaponry that will strike at anyone sending hostile energy. Ideally, a good shield matrix is a combination of all of these things.

When creating a shield, always try to draw on imagery from nature. The closer to a natural pattern something is, the fewer ripples it makes on the fabric of being (Wyrd), the less it stands out, the less energy it requires, and the more difficult it is for an enemy to locate. A good example would be a mountain shield that treats incoming hostile energy as wind. If wind hits the mountain, it doesn't move the mountain; the mountain splits the wind, dispersing it to either side. This is an example of what Clan Tashlin calls "pattern magic"—magic drawn from naturally occurring patterns found in nature. The goal here is to be as effective as possible while wasting as little energy as possible and, more importantly, attracting as little attention as possible.

Shields for mediums

As noted in the chapter on gifts, mediums have etheric/ astral bodies that are not strongly connected to their physical bodies. This makes it easy for entities to come in. While this can be a useful gift when it's controlled, uncontrolled it can drive the medium to mental breakdown. This can be a difficult gift to shield, particularly if the medium isn't owned by a specific Deity (such ownership can provide immense protection).

Firstly, ground and center often, as though your life depended upon it. Secondly, call regularly upon your ancestors. Set up an ancestral altar and work with it regularly. On it, place pictures of them, objects that belonged to them, a copy of your genealogy—anything that calls to you, really. Light candles, burn incense, and offer fresh water and, on special occasions, food and wine to your dead. Talk to them, make them a part of your family, and tell them what's occurring in your life. Ask them to watch over you. (This alone can provide powerful protection for an untrained medium.) Before anything else, I would encourage a medium to get his or her ancestral house in order. You don't need to know their names to call upon them.

They know you. If you're adopted, you have two sets of ancestors you can call upon: your birth ancestors and your adopted ones. Ancestors can also include people not related to you by blood but who were mentors or teachers in some way. Take advantage of this!

Thirdly, shield the gift channel. Most mediums, when they interact with spirits, can usually feel a spirit attempting to enter their body at a particular place at the back of their head. This is the port to shield. This special shielding should be an integral part of any psychic shield. And finally, raise a good, solid shield matrix. It doesn't have to be terribly complex, but it should definitely include at least two, maybe three, strong layers.

Camouflaging

There are a number of reasons to camouflage a shield. The first one is that it's a walking advertisement that you are a person who possesses power. Therefore it can attract unwanted, annoying, or even dangerous attention from discarnate entities, elementals, and other magicians. A shield can also make people around you uncomfortable, even those who are not particularly gifted. It can feel as though you are blocking them or pushing them away (which you are, just not in the way they think). Those with sight are able to see shields; they can even deduce from its construction just how powerful and skilled you are. From a tactical standpoint, this is to be avoided.

Chameleon shield

To cast a chameleon shield, call up the energy around you just as you would with a bubble shield, but set its pattern to reflect your surroundings. Tell it that it's chameleon skin. It should pick up on and assume the frequency of your surroundings. In essence, the external skin of the shield becomes like a movie screen, playing an image of whatever you're doing and wherever you are. A similar effect can be achieved by setting the shield to be faceted like dozens of reflective prisms. The downside of this is that if someone with sight looks at you, they won't see you. There are some people who have a talent for shielding and who might manage to shield this well without any training at all, but they are extremely rare.

Notice-me-nots

There are a number of ways to cast this type of shield, but it works best when done with a bit of projective empathy. One way to do it is to create a picture in your mind of how you want to be seen. Imbue and reinforce this image with emotion, a projective empathic force, as if you were stating to the world, "Nothing to see here." And then project that thought around yourself. You want to make people's eyes glance over and off of you. They literally will not see you. The shield should be set to perpetually "broadcast" this "notice-me-not" directive, and/or whatever image you wish to present.

If you're extremely gifted, you can set this shield to mimic the energy field of a regular, everyday, un-gifted person. This is a delicate thing, though, and I've always found it difficult to maintain. Keep in mind that this type of shield may waver or give way in the face of strong emotions. That's because you're doing more than just creating a shield: you're actively affecting the minds of those people who may encounter you. It's a combination of telepathic and empathic suggestion, carried, in part, by the energy raised for the shield itself.

Another useful notice-me-not provides us with a good example of what is called "pattern magic" at work. Create a simple energetic shield, just as you would for a bubble or mirror shield. Tell the shield that it is a rock and that all incoming emotions, energy, and even people you encounter are water, water rushing in a stream in which the rock is situated. Set this shield to extend a bit farther than normal from your aura. The "water" will hit the "rock" and part before it, just as real water would before a large rock in a rushing stream. This is a good shield to create and keep latent, hidden in your shield matrix or even your ground. Just tuck it away. You can activate it when you are in large crowds or feeling particularly battered empathically.

A Note on Layering Shields

A good shield matrix is comprised of at least two layers. It's important to make sure that the layers are complementary and that they work well together. I would not, for instance, layer a fire shield and a wind shield on top of each other for the simple reason that fire tends to feed upon wind, and there is too great a chance that these two shields would merge into one, thus defeating the purpose of layering. Give serious thought to how the various layers will interact. What will each layer do to incoming energy? This can tell you which order will be most favorable and effective.

When you're first learning how to shield, raise one good, solid shield and work with it for a while. When you're comfortable with it, and when you can go a day without having to check it, add a second layer. Work with the two of them for a while until you're absolutely comfortable with them and they remain strong and integrated. Then add a third. Don't rush the process. It's better to take a bit of time than to risk having weak or unstable shields.

Finally, as with anything else, the key to good shields is practice. Using one's psi-gifts and working actively with energy is very similar to building up a muscle. It takes time and consistent, repetitive practice. So be patient with yourself and don't shirk on the practice part.

4

Warding

I will be the first to admit that my working style is an eclectic blend of various styles, from hoodoo to pure energy-work, psionics to ceremonial magic, with a healthy dose of runes and elemental magic thrown in for good measure, and nowhere is this more strongly reflected than in how I ward a house. This largely stems from the fact that I'm primarily a trouble-shooter, which has made me extremely pragmatic. If something works, I'll use it. It's as simple as that. So the techniques that I suggest for warding a house tend to be equal parts ceremonial, hoodoo, and plain old nasty folk magic (and if you think witch bottles aren't nasty, read the recipe that follows!). Though I am a Northern Traditionalist and a fairly accomplished rune-worker, I do not often use runes in warding my home, for the simple reason that runes are living spirits and require negotiation, offerings, and consistent attention to insure the integrity of their proffered wards. Not everyone is up to that ongoing process. It's always best to keep things as simple as possible, especially in energy-work and magic. To this end, I incorporate a number of talismans and charms in warding a house for one reason and one reason alone: they are effective. Best of all, almost anyone can use them. Stones and herbs, after all, have their own energy. Creating a warding charm using these things is almost like a chemistry experiment: combine the right ingredients in the right order and voila, you'll get the right result. I'm also very lazy and I loathe the thought of wasting energy, so if I can accomplish up to a third of my house warding by using the inherent energies of natural tools such as stones, herbs, and resins, that's a substantial amount of energy I don't have to expend. This is all to the good. It's economical and efficient. Both magic and energy-work are about acquiring power, and that starts by not wasting it.

Good psychic self-defense begins with personal maintenance—the grounding, centering, and shielding that we've already discussed. The next step in this process is learning to ward one's space. Space-keeping, as the mother of a magician friend of mine calls it, is essential for energy-workers. Just as we cannot allow ourselves to be attacked from within—by untrained, unmanaged gifts; by excess, ungrounded energies; or by our own lack of self-discipline—so too must we create safe, well-managed spaces without. "As above, so below" has a corollary: "as within, so without." This means that after setting up your personal shields, the next most important thing to do is to establish good house wards. This does for your home what shielding does for your person. What constitutes a "good" house ward is a very subjective thing. It will depend, in part, on the type of work one is doing. Similar to a good personal shield, a good house ward is flexible and built to accommodate the energy-worker who specializes in healing working and living space that is energetically lends itself to creating an atmosphere of . A diviner might require working space against astral entities or the spirits of the dead. A working magician may prefer the security of heavy, multilayered wards. It's a matter of personal need and personal taste, things which may vary as one develops greater skill or finds one's client base changing.

Creating a good house ward has three parts: cleaning the space, warding the space, and creating the appropriate ambiance within that ward. Effective wards are really no more difficult to build and maintain than personal shields, and that's something to keep in mind as we go over these techniques. The benefit of house wards lies in the fact that so much of it can be done with talismans; also, because they are restricted to one place, they tend to require less energy to maintain their strength.

For those who own their own homes outright, warding should be a breeze. For the rest of us, you will find that as you slowly pay off your mortgage, your ability to thoroughly ward your home will grow stronger almost of its own accord. There is a tremendous power in the right of ownership. I first realized this when my teacher bought her own house, moving from a cramped and tiny New York City apartment to a spacious home in upstate New York. She bought her home outright and the closer she came to signing the contract, the weaker her apartment wards became. By the time she actually owned the house and began moving in, a relatively tenacious ward was already in place. The ones in her apartment had become bare bones; in fact, they'd almost fallen apart. Eventually we realized that they'd transferred themselves to her home. This is when we came to understand that the right of ownership provides its own protection. This is a good place to start. Know where the boundaries of your territory begin and end. Know what is yours by right. This is what you have an obligation to maintain but this is also what has obligations to you.

This is not to say that one cannot effectively ward an apartment. I do. My teacher did so for years, and I know many skillful energy-workers and magicians who do so now. If you live in an apartment, that space is yours by right for as long as you rent that apartment, take proper care of it, and pay your rent on time. The same warding principles apply, albeit to a lesser degree than they would with full-out ownership. In other words, you'll have to do a bit more groundwork.

Begin your process of house warding by actually cleaning your house. Do this regularly. This is first and foremost a means of honoring your space. More to the point, however, clutter collects stagnant and sometimes even negative energy. Ideally, to honor your home, you should be doing this thoroughly mundane cleaning weekly, at least. This should be done as a gift to the home itself. In warding a home, you don't just want to ward out negative and harmful energies; you also want to bring peace and harmony into your home, which is best done by actively managing the internal energy of the space. After all, energy, like nature, abhors a vacuum.

Next, make an offering to your house spirits. In Norse Tradition, these are called *Vaettir* (singular: *vaet;* also, *wight* in Anglo-Saxon writings). This is an all-purpose term for pretty much any unseen spirit that's not a ghost. Vaettir are intimately connected to the elements, to the energies of a home, and to certain places and organic things. They're somewhat analogous to the Japanese *kami*.[1] Being on friendly terms with your house spirits can go a long way toward keeping the energy of a house clean, harmonious, and well-balanced. I suggest setting aside a special bowl that is only used for Vaettir offerings. Traditional offerings include alcohol, milk and bread, or milk and honey, but you may get a strong feeling to offer something else. If you do, go with that feeling and make regular weekly offerings. If you bake or cook regularly, make it a practice to give them the first bite or slice of whatever you're making. You can even ask them to help you keep the house pleasant and free of malignant energies.

After completing these two steps, clean your house magically. There are numerous ways to do this and many of them will be covered in the next chapter on cleansings. I would suggest using a combination of at least two methods in order to get the job done thoroughly. There's one thing to watch out for: when you are cleaning your house magically, crack a window or leave the door open. You want to drive stagnant and/or negative energy out, and it's important to give it somewhere to go. Always keep in mind that energy doesn't just go away. It has to have somewhere to go. If you are a priest/ess, gythia, godhi, or other clergy, or if you know a clergyperson whose faith is compatible your own, it doesn't hurt to have him or her come in and bless your home, as well. If you can do it yourself, all the better; combine it with the house warding. When I ward my space, I often also bless and consecrate it. Negative beings will be deterred by the blessing.

Once your home has been thoroughly cleaned both magically and physically, you should to cast a ward around your home just as you would around yourself. It's very important to give this ward (which should be the primary ward on your home) an external power source. I also suggest giving it expression in a particular object somewhere in the house. Let's look at how this is done.

The Energy Ward

First, select a focus. I use a piece of tiger's eye (my preferred stone, one that I like and resonate very strongly with) the size of my head as the temporal and physical focus for my house wards.[2] This stone occupies a nook in a fairly central spot in my apartment. In every room, there is also a smaller piece of tiger's eye, usually concealed, to "hook into" and bolster the charm. Stones work well as anchoring points for energy: they're stable, solid, and hold energy very well. Stones are actually living things but they age and change so slowly that the human eye cannot see it. They age and grow at a far different pace than we do.

Once I've selected my stones and positioned them around my home, I send down mental tendrils into whatever or wherever I want to draw the energy from. I personally draw my house wards from several of the nine Norse worlds, from which I have permission to draw. You will have to select accessible power sources. There is nothing wrong with drawing from the earth itself; however, I caution against tying a ley line or node into one's house wards, as this source of power can become rapidly depleted, which isn't good for you or the land. The land is a living thing, too, one that supports and nourishes us. Ideally we should all strive to do as little harm as possible to it.

Once I have selected my power source, I tie those tendrils of mental energy into my focus stone so that energy rushes in and builds within the stone itself. A house ward must encompass all directions, so I start to thread that energy out and around the perimeter of the house, the ceilings, and the floors using the smaller foci to lock the energy into its desired shape. As I do this, I tell the energy strongly what type of shield it will be, what it will be defending against, and how it should react. I also tell it where it will continue to draw its power from. After this, I make sure that the energy is a.) feeding into the focus strongly and evenly, and b.) feeding into the ward itself equally strongly and evenly. It's important that there not be any holes or weak spots. Then I seal it with a symbol of power (this, too, is a matter of personal inclination and choice) and a drop of my own blood drawn with a diabetic lancet.[3]

If I intend to tie more than one layer of shielding into the focus stone, I repeat this process and then consciously integrate the various layers, making sure every layer is compatible with the next. This is done by willing the result, telling the energy what it is and what it should do, and then stepping back and seeing how it feels. I also tell my shields what other types of energy they can feed upon in addition to their power source—for example, storms, incoming attacks, ambient emotions from your surroundings, and so on.[4] There is one important caveat here: a house ward should *never* be set to draw energy continuously from the person who creates it. You are not its energy source. It must be completely separate from you; otherwise it can be like having a constantly bleeding wound that will lead to weakness, malaise, exhaustion, even illness.

If you don't want to use a physical focus, you can just as easily tie the ward into the electrical lines within your home. I live in an old building, though, and I felt a bit paranoid about putting any added stress on the wiring. You could also run the energy shield through the plumbing, as pipes are perfectly shaped to be used as conduits for energy. But again, in older buildings this may not be the best idea.

This energy matrix is your basic and most fundamental house ward. You create it by doing almost exactly what you would do to create a personal shield, save that a house ward is tied more strongly into a stationary power source.

Herbs, Camphor, and Vinegar

Once you have your basic energy matrix constructed and properly functioning, there are a few other simple things you can do to amp up the power and efficacy of your wards. Remember I said that I liked using hoodoo and folk magic in my house wards? Well, this is where that comes into play. To begin with, I suggest putting a camphor square in every corner of your bedroom. Camphor is a powerful substance that will block a great deal of spirit manifestation. For this reason, if ancestral veneration is part of your practice, do not do this in the room that holds your ancestral altar—it can be unpleasant for them. Camphor evaporates, so you will have to change the squares monthly. If you can't find camphor squares, use moth balls. I don't do this in every room in my house, however—only my bedroom. It's good to have one room to which you can retire that is completely and thoroughly sealed off from external beings and energies. (However, this will not block a Deity.) I find that the dreaming state is very strongly connected to the astral plane. When we dream, sometimes we travel into that energy plane and that can open doors that allow us to be influenced by spirits or certain types of Vaettir. Sealing your bedroom helps ensure that these bothersome spirits can't come back with you into this plane, through the doorway of your dreamwork.[5]

In addition to the camphor, it can be very beneficial to place small cups of red vinegar in each room of your house. My grandmother used to do this when I was very young. She had learned this trick from her grandmother who was a spiritualist. She only knew that it kept the house clean. It wasn't until years later as an adult that I learned from a hoodoo teacher that it's an old trick of folk magic designed to prevent negative spirit manifestation. I have found it to be very effective. As with the camphor, some people have trouble tolerating the smell of the vinegar. I find that placing the small containers several feet above head height (on the tops of cupboards, for instance) usually remedies this problem. I recommend changing them every week.

Once you have done all of this, your home may feel clean but rather sterile. One solution is to light a few candles, asking the spirits of Fire to bless and consecrate your home. Play some of your favorite music and allow it to resonate throughout the house or apartment. Music can change the ambience of a room, and changing the ambience changes the energy. In addition, some people are very sensitive to color and respond well to color therapy. My teacher used this knowledge in decorating her house: she chose warm, welcoming neutrals and then carefully selected artwork to create a homey, inviting feel. I did much the same thing but on a smaller scale. Think about the space you are in. Consciously honor that space. The way you choose to decorate your home can have tremendous impact on how the energy within those walls feels. This is one of the guiding principles of feng shui. You don't have to be a feng shui master to incorporate these principles into your dwelling; just pay attention to how changes to your space (no matter how small) make you feel, and act accordingly.

If the energy of your home still feels sterile, agitated, or uncomfortable, a little herbal action might help change that. Two herbs in particular—marjoram and basil—are excellent for bringing peace to a home, for lightening the energy, and for helping make it inhospitable to negative influences. That's really what this part of house warding is about—making the energy inside your home inhospitable to negative, jagged, or outright malignant energy. These two herbs, either used alone or combined in roughly equal portions, are excellent tools to have on hand. I often travel on business, and I've been known to take a container of basil with me. I pour out a tablespoon or two into a cup and put it in the four corners of my hotel room (yes, I throw it out in the mornings before I leave to spare housekeeping). It does wonders for keeping the space clean. At home, you need not risk attracting roaches by keeping the herbs out. Instead, make a strong infusion of both together. This is done by pouring boiling water over two to four tablespoons of each of the herbs and allowing it to steep for 20 minutes.[6] Strain the herbs out and walk clockwise around your house, aspersing the ceiling, walls, and floor. Basil and marjoram are "happy" herbs, meaning that the frequency of their energy feels happy and pleasant to us, and will create feelings of harmony and contentment when used in this way. Basil also has some mild protective qualities.

Once your wards are up and running and the energy inside your home feels comfortable, it's time to attack two of the weakest spots in any house: the threshold and all primary reflective surfaces (windows and mirrors). A threshold is a weak spot because so many people are constantly crossing it, bringing with them disparate and often undisciplined energies.[7] Windows and mirrors are dangerous because they can serve as doorways for certain types of beings and also for magic. They can also cause the energy in the house to flow strangely or unpleasantly. Fortunately, both are fairly easy to ward.

Warding the Threshold

There are a number of ways to properly warding a threshold. All of them can be incorporated organically into the design of your home. They don't have to look strange or out of place. Use the techniques that feel comfortable and adapt them as needed for your personal circumstances. However, you need to be fully behind what you do—emotionally, mentally, and spiritually.

You could hang something made of iron over your door. I have an old horse shoe. Their folkloric propensity for bringing good luck stems more from the natural ability of iron to ward off certain kinds of energy than it does from the shape of the iron. You could also hang a blessing charm (recipe on page 113) over the door. I actually have numerous charms hanging over my door, each with its own specific function. Don't feel the need to limit yourself to just one.[8]

Another method is to mix red ochre, dragon's blood, a few drops of your own blood, and enough water to make a paste and paint the following protective sigils on your door: an aegishamr in the middle of the door (or a pentacle, if you are Wiccan or generic Pagan), and the runes Tiewaz, Algiz, and Othila down either side of the door. Add whatever other protective symbols you prefer. You can then go ahead and paint over these sigils. If you would rather not paint sigils on your door, you may use a blended oil or even blessed water, both of which should be redone monthly.

My favorite method is a Lukumi protection charm that I learned from a Santero friend of mine. Take a length of chain and affix nails and pins to it. Call upon the warrior God of your choice to bless and charge the chain, imbuing it with protective power. Really charge the hell out of it. Fill it with as much protective and defensive energy as you can. Take a cigar and inhale the smoke, blowing it out upon the chain several times. Then take a mouthful of rum and spit it out on the chain to "feed" it. Do this several times. Hang this chain over the lintel of your front door on the inside. I call upon Heimdall, asking Him to guard my threshold when I do this. Originally Ogoun would have been called for this charm, but I suggest adapting it to whatever warrior Deity you most resonate with. I feed the chain and make offerings to Heimdall fairly regularly.

Another method involving hanging small knives on either side of your door. They should be charged to cut any offensive, harmful, and/or malignant incoming energy. Having taught martial arts for a number of years, I collect weapons, so no one looks twice at the spear resting in the corner behind my door or the Japanese swords neatly displayed on the rack near my door.

Regularly asperse the door and the threshold itself with blessed water or water with a few drops of protective oil blended in. Because I worked with a Santero for a few years, I got into the habit of using certain colognes, such as Kolonia Sandalo, or Kolonia 1800, both of which are readily available at most botanicas.[9] Keep salt regularly sprinkled across the outside threshold of your door, as well. Regularly do the pentacle warding charm (given on page 112) on inside of the front door. And finally, when you are having people over, particularly if you don't know them very well, put a big bowl of water behind the door or as near to the door as you can. It will absorb negative energy as people enter. You can pour Kolonia Sandalo into the water to give it a bit of extra oomph if you wish.

There is one caveat regarding these techniques: some of the wards (the threshold chain, for instance) will have to be "fed" regularly; others will need to be repeated often. Sigils painted on the door will need to be "blooded" with a few drops pricked from your finger every couple of months. If they're drawn with water or oil, they need to be redone monthly or even weekly. The pentacle warding charm should be repeated at least monthly, if not weekly.

Wards should not attract attention, so it's best to camouflage them just as you would your shields. Such camouflage can be done one of two ways: you can either cast another external energy ward designed to conceal the others, or, if you have facility at working Wyrd (which will be discussed in the chapter

on energy-work), you can grab the fabric
and pull it over you. Think of this as grab
night and wrapping it around you like a cl
rectly, it will render your wards invisible. Th   .~ is
that there will be an energetic hole where some ...ng ought to
be; thus, this type of concealment only works well in a city or
in crowds, where the sheer mass of bodies effectively conceals
the concealment. Camouflage shields, particularly the prism
shield described in the section on personal shields, will also
work very well for concealing a house ward. More so even than
for personal shields, it's important for safety's sake that house
wards look as unprepossessing as possible. In my opinion, the
best type of concealment is to cast an external ward specifically designed to make the home look as boring and normal
as possible. You raise the energy, shape it, tie it into the rest
of your wards, give it a power source, and, focusing your will
and intent, tell it what it will be and what it is supposed to do.
When you come down to it, that's the foundation for almost all
energy-work: focused will.

Warding Windows and Mirrors

Unwarded windows and mirrors make excellent doorways
and can provide entry points for unwanted negative magic. I
prefer to have as few mirrors as possible in my home because
they tend to create strange energy flows, or magnify and agi-
tate energy in ways that can be uncomfortable. Still, it's rare to
find someone who is willing to forego all mirrors, and really,
there's no need if they're properly shielded. It is of utmost importance that both be strongly warded when securing your
home. Unfortunately, this is a step that is all too often forgot-
ten. In my opinion, mirrors are more problematic than windows. I ward both by means of the following two charms.

Pentacle warding charm

The strongest charm that I know is one I learned roughly 15 years ago from my first teacher, who said it was based on the work of Dion Fortune. It is very ceremonial, but I have adapted it for my own usage as I am a hard polytheist, and the original all-encompassing Goddess and God attributions didn't sit well with me. My adaptation is given in brackets in the third step:

1. Choose an oil that you like. I usually use whatever I have on hand, though there are numerous protective oils available. A good dragon's blood oil would be perfect for this. I usually use lavender, largely because I almost always have it around the house. Cedar oil, which is an oil of consecration, would be ideal for this working.

2. Center and ground yourself, then begin by raising energy, drawing it up through your grounding channel and into your hands. Hold the oil between your hands and send that energy into the oil. Mentally focus on filling the oil with as much energy as it will hold.[10]

3. Pour some of the oil onto your fingers. You are going to be drawing a pentacle, a five pointed star. Starting at the lower left corner, draw a line to the top center point of the star saying, "By the Name that is above all Names, by the Great Goddess and Her Mighty Lord [by the Great Goddess Frigga and Her Mighty Lord Odin]."

4. Draw from the center point to the lower right corner, saying, "I banish all influences and seeds of evil."

5. Draw from the lower right corner to the upper left corner, saying, "I lay upon them a spell of holiness and power."

6. Draw from top left corner across to top right, saying, "That they be bound fast as with chains."

7. Draw from the top right corner to the lower left corner, saying, "And cast into the outer darkness."

8. Touch the center of the pentacle, saying, "That they trouble not this servant of the Gods."

Do this on your door and on every window and mirror in your house. Then, using the same oil, I like to draw either the rune Algiz or the rune Ior on the windows, mirrors, and doors. You could also hang a blessing charm over each window and over the door. I do not hang such a charm over the mirrors, though you could if they were special cause for concern.

Blessing charm

This charm is for peace, harmony, and protection within the home. First, take three runes—Tiewaz, Algiz, and Othila. Chant over them and anoint them with the ochre/dragon's blood/blood mixture that I described previously. You may use actual rune tiles or draw the runes on pieces of paper. Then, put the runes in a green pouch and combine them with the following ingredients:

- 3 pinches of basil (for protection)
- 1 large pinch of marjoram (for harmony and peace)
- 1 cross stone (for grounding and stability)
- 1 small jalap root (for power)
- 1 tonka bean (for pleasant relationships and luck)
- 1 garnet (for protection)

- ๑๏ 1 black tourmaline (for absorbing and shunting negative energy away from the home)
- ๑๏ A piece of turquoise (to ward off evil)

Charge the pouch strongly, imprinting it with the idea of peace and harmony. Draw the power symbol of your choice over the pouch to seal it. Hang it up and do not open it (opening it will disperse the energy). Should the time come when you need to discard it, take it down, open it, and scatter the contents. I recommend either tossing them over your shoulder at a crossroads (intersection), throwing them into running water, or burying them. I think it's important to be respectful of our working tools, which are, in a sense, our allies. Properly disposing of these things is just as important as properly crafting them.

This is the recipe that I use most often, but there is no need to feel that you must limit yourself to this particular charm. There are a number of good books on the market listing the magical properties of plants, herbs, roots, and stones. Personally, I highly recommend Catherine Yronwode's *Hoodoo Herb and Root Magic*. Scott Cunningham's *Crystal, Gem, and Metal Magic* isn't bad, either. Once you have a good compendium, you can make your own talismans. The idea is to combine ingredients of compatible energies so that the combined whole produces the desired effect. I encourage experimentation here.

Witch bottles

I love witch bottles. I really do. They're nasty, easy to make, and very effective. Witch's bottles date back at least to the early 18th century. (They've been found buried in the foundations of houses from this period in both England and the United States.) These charms are designed to absorb and disperse negative, malignant, and harmful energies. The power is derived from the combination of ingredients.

Get a good, sturdy mason jar. Once this thing is sealed you do not, under any circumstances, want to open it again. In the jar combine as many of the following ingredients as you can come up with:

- Nine rusty nails
- Bent pins
- Rue
- Red and black pepper
- Cayenne pepper
- House dust
- Tangled bits of string
- Broken glass
- Broken mirror pieces
- Old razor blades
- Barbed wire
- Thorns
- Whitethorn (hawthorn)
- Blackthorn
- Dragon's blood
- Jalap root
- Any other baneful herbs available
- Small fishing hooks (optional)

Now urinate in the bottle. This is an absolutely necessary part of the spell. Symbolically you are both marking your territory and, more importantly, pissing on your enemies. Energetically, it makes a powerful statement.[11] Add enough regular tap water to fill the jar and seal it securely. Pour black candle wax over the top of the jar and around its mouth, sealing it even more securely.

Looking at the lists of substances that one can include in a witch's bottle might evoke a good bit of curiosity. One might ask, Why copper? Why bent nails? Why red thread? Since the Renaissance (and probably long before that), those interested in the occult have attempted to compile concordances and compendiums attributing planetary and elemental influences to lists of substances. For instance, the herb mugwort is considered an herb of Fire (which is interesting because it is used today in the Chinese medical practice of *moxibustion*). The stone hematite is associated both with Earth and Fire, which complements its use as a grounding tool. But these attributions were very likely drawn from folk knowledge of the time. Why bent nails? Well, probably because they were at one time made of iron, and iron in folklore was often used to drive away evil. Why copper? I could speculate that copper is an excellent conductor of energy, but whether or not our ancestors knew that is debatable. Sadly, the answers to most of these questions have been lost to history. We use these substances because they have specific energy resonances or attributions comparable to the purpose of the charm. And, because they are effective. Basically, we use them because they work.

Ancient occultists and energy-workers might also have been familiar with something called the Doctrine of Signatures. This is a theory of medicine and herbalism that is commonly thought to date from the 16th century, but in actuality dates back at least to the time of Galen, circa C.E. 120. The basic tenet of the doctrine is that you can determine the medicinal action of a plant or herb by looking at its shape and color. For instance, goldenrod was once prescribed to treat jaundice, because one of the symptoms of jaundice is a yellowing of the skin and goldenrod has a bright yellow flower. The Doctrine was later expanded upon by no less a mental heavyweight than Paracelsus. Its medical influence continued until well into the late 19th century. Although modern medicine and modern herbalism have disregarded this doctrine as superstition, its influence on herbalism (and, by extension, root-work and hoodoo) has been undeniable. From an energy-worker's perspective, it is a form of sympathetic magic: the part that represents the whole can affect the whole. Remember, there was a time when folk traditions and what passed for medicine were not that far apart.

There are several modern compendiums on the market that are an excellent place to start researching herbs and various substances. It's good to have a couple of these on hand, because they are extremely useful when it comes to constructing a charm such as a witch bottle. I recommend Catherine Yronwode's *Hoodoo Herb and Root Magic*, *Cunningham's Encyclopedia of Crystal, Gem, and Metal Magic*, and *The Master Book of Herbalism* by Paul Beyerl.

There are two ways to dispose of a witch bottle; I prefer the second. The first is to bury it outside; the second is to hide it in your house somewhere where you won't have to see it regularly. I stuck mine way back in the corner of my bathroom behind a cabinet. Once you make one, put it away and leave it alone. Don't even think about it again. Trust it to do its job. Should you ever move, you have a bit of a quandary—should you leave the bottle? If not, how do you safely dispose of what is essentially a magical bio-hazard?[12] Above all else, do not open the bottle. I suggest wrapping it in silk.[13] Try to avoid touching it with your bare hands. Put it in a bowl and fill that bowl with salt. Let it sit for a week or two. Then, take the bottle out and either bury it or throw it into running water. (Ask permission from the land and/or water spirits first. They may not want energetic waste tossed in their environs.) Otherwise, if you have access to a fire or a forge, burn it. The glass will explode or melt, and that's okay. Fire purifies by its very nature. Once a witch bottle is made, however, it's really best to never move it. Witch bottles are often found stashed inside the foundations of homes or between their walls. I believe the reason for this is that they are so energetically hazardous to handle. If you must handle one in order to dispose of it, take a cleansing bath afterward.

Some sources advocate adding a bit of your own blood to the bottle. I generally don't bother with this. Although blood that has been drawn for this purpose is generally a powerful spell ingredient, I haven't found that omitting it from a witch bottle impacts the efficacy of the charm at all. In fact, I think adding it could give whatever negative energies it captures a definitive link to you. The urine is sufficient to "key" the bottle to your protection, and the act alone is symbolically charged to put you in control of the energy.

A further note on the use of blood in spells: With the exception of certain fertility charms and one nasty hoodoo love charm, blood used in magic should be drawn with intent. Menstrual blood doesn't count. It's waste blood and thus lacks the power of intentionally drawn blood. It is not life-blood; it is blood that was meant to nourish life but was then expelled from the body. There's no effort and thus no intent in its expulsion, nor is it highly charged energetically as living blood is.

Window bottles

I like to think of window bottles as modified witch bottles. Although they will trap and disperse any incoming negative energy, they don't have the nasty feel that a well-made witch bottle will have, and they are easy to clean energetically. They're also much prettier and good to hang in windows. Basically they function as conduits: energy is drawn in and shunted elsewhere, but in a much cleaner fashion than with a witch bottle. However, they are not as effective.

Acquire a few pretty bottles in various colors. Flea markets, yard sales, and antique stores are all good places to look. Put the following ingredients in each jar:

- ෨෨ A thin coil of copper wire
- ෨෨ Tangled red thread
- ෨෨ Bent pins

Then, fill them with water, seal them, and hang them in your windows. I've known some people who just use the thread and/or the copper. I've found all variations on this charm to be equally effective. Again, you do not want to open these bottles once they've been sealed. In the event that one explodes, it means it has taken a powerful incoming attack for you. If this happens, you may want to increase and strengthen your house wards and take the necessary steps to ward off attack.

War Water

War water is a floor wash. You're actually going to be washing any hardwood, tile, or linoleum floors in your home, the threshold of your door, your front steps, and anywhere else you think necessary with this mixture. This is not something that I suggest using regularly. It's a very intense charm and can feel very "hot" and "heavy" within a home. This is something to use when you feel you might be under magical or energetic attack.

First, take a bucket of water and add a cup of ammonia. Then blend the following ingredients in a large jar and add one cup of the mixture to the bucket of water and ammonia:

- Pinch of salt
- 1 tsp. saltpeter
- Pinch of black pepper
- 1–2 Tbs. of cayenne
- 9 rusty nails
- 1 piece jalap root
- Handful of crushed mint
- 3 pinches dragon's blood
- Urine
- Water to top off the jar

I recommend making this and keeping it in a jar and then adding a cup as needed to the ammonia and water blend. The urine is essential. Again, you are symbolically pissing on your enemies and establishing dominance while marking your space. It's okay to substitute: if you don't have access to jalap or saltpeter, add more pepper or other strong spices. If you don't have rusty nails, use regular nails. They'll rust soon enough.

Uncrossing Charm

This is something I like to do every new moon. It is a traditional uncrossing charm that will banish a good deal of low-level negative energy sent your way. I've found that people can send negative energy out without even realizing it. Most people aren't really conscious of what's going on with their internal energy. Emotions and stress—especially irritation, jealousy, or anger—can leak out. This is one of the origins of *malochia*, or the evil eye. So just because negative energy is coming your way doesn't mean that you're under a curse or being attacked on purpose. Sometimes these things just happen as part of one's day-to-day interactions with people. For this charm, you will need the following ingredients:

- ∞ A large grey candle that can be removed from its glass (a "seven-day candle")
- ∞ A nail to carve a sigil into the candle with
- ∞ A lancet
- ∞ Dragon's blood powder

Carve this sigil on the candle. (Although it's better to do it right on the candle, if you are unable to find a removable candle, draw it with a marker on the glass.) You can carve your name and astrological sign on the candle, as well. If you have a personal sigil, as some magicians do, use that instead. Prick your finger with the lancet and put a few drops of your own blood in the center of the sigil. Rub the carvings and the wick with dragon's blood powder. Charge the candle, holding it between your hands and filling it with energy. When you feel that the candle can take no more, seal the energy in by tracing the sigil of your choice over it (I was taught to use a pentacle). Now light the candle and allow it to burn down all the way. If the candle is in a glass holder, you can put the whole thing in a metal pot of water when you're not in the house. That way, if the glass cracks, the water will put out the flame. If you must blow the candle out, just relight it with focused intent at a later time.

The Lesser Banishing Pentagram (LBP)

There are a number of magical cleansing rituals that are very useful to know, most notably the lesser banishing pentagram. This is a Kabbalistic rite common to certain branches of ceremonial magic. It was one of the first protection rituals I learned and remains a potent tool in my arsenal. If you're uncomfortable invoking the Hebraic names, don't use it. I'm including the version I learned here for thoroughness. It invokes four different names or titles of the Hebrew God and the four archangels. I also believe this should be sung, galdred, or chanted for maximum power.

Begin with the Kabbalistic cross. As you stand facing east, center yourself. Extend your right hand, palm up, out in front of you above your forehead. Draw power into your hand. See and feel it gathering there in a glowing, golden sphere. Bring that power in and touch your forehead, intoning:

"Atah" [to you be]

Touch your breast bone, intoning:

"Malkuth" [the kingdom]

Touch your right shoulder, intoning:

"Ve Geburah" [the power]

Touch your left shoulder, intoning:

"Ve Gedulah" [the glory]

Cross your arms over your chest intoning:

"Le Olam, Amin." [forever and ever, so be it]

This seals the aura.

Next, draw the pentagrams. Facing east again, starting at
the lower left corner and drawing up to the middle point, draw
a five-pointed star. (I actually go from the floor to as high as
I can reach so that the process of doing the LBP becomes a
full-body experience, almost a dance. In this way, I am a better conduit for the energy that I'm raising.) Then point to the
center of the star and intone the sacred name:

"Yod He Vod He."

Turn south and make the same pentagram, intoning:

"Adonai."

Turn west and make the pentagram, intoning:

"Eheieh."

Turn north and make the pentagram, intoning:

"Agla."

The first three are Divine names and the last is a contrac-
tion of a Hebraic phrase that means "Thou art mighty forever,
oh Lord." As you draw the pentagrams, see the energy glowing
in the air. Next, turn east again and call upon the archangels.
Extend your arms out in a cross and intone:

"Before me stands Raphael,

Behind me stands Gabriel,

On my right hand stands Michael,

On my left hand stands Uriel,

Above and below me shine the six-pointed star,

And around me flame the pentacles.

May their light now descend."

Repeat the drawing of the pentagrams and intoning of sacred names from east to north. Close with the Kabbalistic cross.

When one is just starting out, it's a good idea to do some sort of protective rite, such as the LBP, every night. When these rituals are done with proper focus, their protective power will accrue, building up a reservoir in your home. This is an advantage in working any type of cleansing or protective magic.

Warding Your Vehicle

Just as you ward your house, you also need to ward your vehicle. In fact, I would say it's even more important to have good protections on a car than on a house, because there is more of a chance of an accident while driving. The easiest way to do this is to cast an energy ward exactly as you would on your home, save that the power in this case comes from the car engine itself. Every time you rev the engine, the ward is fed more power.

Take a piece of horse tail and braid it around a metal ring. Affix it to a small pouch of comfrey and a small piece of tiger's eye. Hang this from the car mirror or keep it in your glove box. Call upon the God or Goddess of your choice (I usually prefer Gna, the messenger Goddess of the Norse and/or Thor, protector of Midgard) to empower it. You may also petition your Gods to send a protective spirit to inhabit your vehicle. Ask the spirit for its name and talk to it. Work with it and develop a relationship with it. I give mine offerings of tobacco by rubbing it on the four corners of my car. I'm an animist so I am comfortable working this way. If you're not an animist or if this feels silly, don't do it; you have to believe in what you're doing or you'll be unraveling your work from within. You must be fully confident in your ability to affect your environment. This is what both energy-work in general, and magic in particular are all about.

5

Cleansing

Cleanliness is next to godliness, and had better come first.
—*Aleister Crowley*

I am a big proponent of an old saying that an ounce of prevention is worth a pound of cure. There is much wisdom in this saying on a purely practical, everyday level, and it holds equally true for those engaged in magic and energy-work. Knowing how to perform an adequate cleansing of one's person is a powerful component of what I like to call psychic hygiene. So much trouble and discontent could be avoided simply by practicing this basic hygiene on a regular, ongoing basis. Of course, I suppose that holds true for our physical health, too. Taking care of ourselves in the first place goes a long way toward keeping us healthy and preventing sickness. In many respects, energy-work functions along similar lines.

A few years after I'd already learned the basics of energy-work, when I was first learning how to practice magic (and seriously determined to developing excellence in the Art), I spent a solid year doing almost nothing but cleansing rituals (mostly the Lesser Banishing

Pentagram and regular cleansing baths, both of which will be touched on in this chapter). That was it. That was the sum total of my occult practice. It was absolutely maddening! Of course, not having that much practical experience in occult matters, I couldn't understand why that was all I was allowed to do. No matter how much I grumbled and complained, my teacher remained firm: grounding, centering, basic shielding, and energetic cleansings *ad nauseum*. I thought I must be the cleanest apprentice in the tri-state area! Years later, I now understand and appreciate the wisdom and pragmatism of my teacher in forcing me to focus on something so seemingly insignificant and mundane. Knowing how to clean your house and your person energetically, and doing so on a regular basis whether you feel you are under energetic attack or not, is one of the best and most essential things you can do for your personal protection and energy maintenance. This holds true not only for magicians but also for psi-talented folks, energy-workers, Reiki practitioners, healers, and anyone who does ritual work. In fact, it's true for everyone. It's a wonderful panacea, not only for energetic nastiness, but for general malaise and stress, as well.

The first round of defense in the war against energetic grime and malignancy is to clean your house. Clutter attracts stagnant energy, and this is only one step away from becoming a breeding ground for negative energy. Before anything else, clean your house thoroughly. Housecleaning is a way of owning and maintaining your space. Indeed, as Fuensanta Arismendi once said to me, "Hold the space against entropy, dirt, neglect, against passivity. In all four corners you have, you hold the space. Upward and downward, you hold the space against chaos. When you clean, you invoke order, purity, and guard sacred space against its opposite. This is what I do every day when I clean the toilet." This is the most fundamental aspect of energy-work, and it is utterly foundational to efficient work. After cleaning oneself and one's space, it's okay to turn to energetic methods such as charms and wards. These things work best, however, when their application rests on a mundanely clean surface.

After your space is clean, one of the most common ways to clean yourself energetically is by cleaning your physical body in a cleansing bath. The cleansing bath uses various combinations of substances in much the same way that creating a magical charm bag does. The combination of energies from the ingredients creates a desired outcome—in this case, the removal of negative energies.

There are two ways to take a cleansing bath: the traditional way and the comfortable way. The traditional method involves making an infusion of herbs and substances, letting it sit and steep, and straining it into a jar when cool. Then you strip down, stand in a tub or shower, and pour the infusion over your head and body. Because it is considered important in some traditions to not wipe the infusion off, you then allow yourself to air dry and dress in clean clothes. If the infusion is warm it isn't so bad, but if it's cold (which it generally is), the process can be unpleasant. The more comfortable way of taking a cleansing bath, and the one I personally prefer, involves adding a cup or two of the requisite infusion to your bathwater and soaking in it. This is also a good option if you live in an apartment that only has a bathtub. Regardless of which you method you use, be sure to douse your head thoroughly.

Here I offer a few common types of cleansing baths. Please don't limit yourself to my recipes alone. Acquire a good magical herbal, or, better yet, take Catherine Yronwode's hoodoo and root-work course (available at *www.luckymojo.com*). Hoodoo stresses cleansing baths almost as much as my first teacher did.

For the record, any combination of cleansing and purifying herbs can be used in a cleansing bath. Combinations of three are popular. (It is also possible to create baths to bring luck, abundance, and happiness into your life, but that is a bit beyond the scope of this book.) I recommend taking at least one cleansing bath per week. There have been times in my magical life when the first thing I did after coming home every single day was to take a cleansing bath. You simply can't do this too often.

ᗊᗊ The Beer Bath ᗊᗊ

My favorite cleansing bath, and one that I try to do at least twice a month, comes from a German folk custom. I'll admit I was dubious about this one at first, but it's one of the most effective cleansing bath recipes I have ever tried—and I've tried a lot of recipes! To use this bath, add a large bottle of dark beer to your bathwater. Soak for at least 10 minutes, being sure to douse every part of your body, including the crown of your head. (Don't worry—the water dilutes the smell of the beer.) If you like, you can add a handful of kosher or sea salt to the bathwater, but this isn't necessary. My grandmother used to recommend this bath to me, telling me it was good for the hair and skin. I suppose it is, but that's not why I do it. Of course, grandma also set out cups of red vinegar all over her house. I never knew why until I studied hoodoo as an adult. Turns out this is a recipe to prevent negative spirit manifestation. She learned it from her grandmother, who was a spiritualist.[1]

ᗊᗊ Apple Cider Vinegar and Salt Bath ᗊᗊ

The very first cleansing bath recipe that I ever learned was equally simple: one cup of apple cider vinegar and a half cup of salt added to the bathwater. Again, soak for at least 10 minutes and be sure to douse everything, including your head. If you have nothing else on hand, a cup of salt alone will do a pretty good job, particularly if you consecrate it first. Hold your hand over the salt and say, "I bless and consecrate you, O creature of earth, that you may cleanse and purify, driving out all malignancy. So mote it be." Feel energy flowing from the earth, through your root, through your hands, and into the salt. Visualize it glowing with cleansing power. Words have immense power in magic, and the simple act of consecration can work wonders. I rarely find the need to consecrate in such a manner, but it is a viable technique nonetheless. Anything that connects a practitioner more strongly to the inherent power of his or her tools is worth considering.

๏๛ White Bath ๛๏

The fact that I use white baths is yet another example of my eclecticism of practice. Although I am not particularly eclectic in my spiritual life, being a Northern Traditionalist, I am very eclectic in my occult life. As an energy-worker, magician, and occultist, I am also extremely pragmatic. If it works, I'll probably use it. In Afro-Caribbean traditions, white baths are associated with Obatala, the Orisha of cleanliness, purity, and order. His name means "king of the white cloth," which symbolizes serenity. White baths are often prescribed to cleanse and purify when practitioners are under stress or magical attack or when they need serenity and clarity returned to their lives.

To make a white bath, you combine a number of white ingredients, as white is Obatala's color. Certain purifying herbs may also be added.[2] The recipe here will probably necessitate a trip to your local botanica. You will also need a white seven-day candle as an offering to Obatala. This bath takes eight days.

Ingredients:

- ᥫ᭡ Quita Maldicion
- ᥫ᭡ Almond leaves
- ᥫ᭡ Cascarilla chalk
- ᥫ᭡ Maravilla (Calendula)
- ᥫ᭡ White flowers of any type
- ᥫ᭡ Milk from four coconuts
- ᥫ᭡ Goat's milk
- ᥫ᭡ Shea butter
- ᥫ᭡ Peppermint
- ᥫ᭡ An extra coconut, split in half

While praying to Obatala and your ancestors, shred the Maldicion into cold water and allow it to steep overnight. Mix the herbs into cold water and let them sit. I recommend letting them soak in jars, which you can then cap. That way you can keep the mixture, easily adding what you need for the bath each night. Sing to Obatala. Pray to Him and ask His blessing, asking Him to lend His power to the bath. Sing or pray to your ancestors and ask them to lend their power and blessing, as well. Sprinkle the cascarilla and white flower petals into the bath right before use on the first of the eight days. Refrigerate the goat's milk and coconut milk (and you must actually crack the coconuts and acquire the milk yourself; do not use canned milk) and add each day to the bath, along with a cup of the herbal mixture.

Before bathing, light the candle in offering to Obatala. Blow it out after your bath each day except the last. While in the bath, rub yourself down with the herbs and leaves from that day's allotment of the mixture. Be sure to douse your head with the bathwater. Before each bath, dust the coconut halves with cascarilla chalk. After the bath cycle is finished, clean yourself with the coconut. Rub it all over yourself, cleansing your aura, all the while offering it to Obatala. After each bath, gather up the remaining leaves in your tub and discard them in a river or ocean. It's disrespectful to just throw them in the garbage. If you don't have access to a large body of water, bury them in the ground.

On the eighth day of the bath, let the candle burn down completely. Gather up all the used herbs in a white cloth and tie it with a red ribbon. Take the bundle and the coconut halves to a white tree (preferably a birch or cotton tree) and leave it there. To thank Obatala for His blessings, take two coconuts covered in cascarilla chalk and eight pennies in a bag (eight is His number) and put them under a white tree or in a bush. Make sure they are hidden from sight.

Energetic baths can be used for many other purposes besides simple cleansing. In fact, a day or so after doing a cleansing bath, it can be quite nice to create an energetic bath to bring about a particular emotional state. Again, a good magical herbal is essential. A calming bath is but one example of the type of bath you can create.

❧ Calming Bath ☙

- ❧ 3–5 sliced oranges
- ❧ Cinnamon sticks
- ❧ Whole cloves
- ❧ White flowers
- ❧ Honey
- ❧ Collonia 1800 Sandalo (available at most botanicas) or your favorite oil or perfume
- ❧ Rum

Let all of this steep for a while in room temperature water. Warm it up but do not bring it to a boil. Add the rum and, while standing in a bath, pour the entire mixture over yourself from the head down. Just bask in the scent.

෬ Seven African Powers Cleansing Bath ෬

This is another bath drawn from Afro-Caribbean practices. At an early stage in my magical training, I worked with a Santeria practitioner from whom I learned a great deal about ancestral veneration, and with whom I often exchanged bath recipes. This was one that he taught me.

- ෬ Strong rosemary infusion
- ෬ Rum
- ෬ Seven-day candle

Light a candle to the Seven African Orisha: Obatala, Ogun, Ellegua, Yemaya, Chango, Oshun, and Oya. Add rum to the rosemary infusion, and add this to your bath each night for seven days. As you bathe, keep the candle going. You may blow it out after each night except the last, when it should be allowed to burn down completely. This is a particularly good bath to use when your energy is being drained and also as a general clearing.

෬ Sweet and Sour Bath ෬

I really like this combination. There's an old axiom that nature abhors a vacuum. With this bath you're cleansing and simultaneously bringing in something positive to fill the space that had been taken up by the negative energy. This bath both breaks up negative influences *and* brings in positive ones.

To break up the negative influences:

- Rue
- Poke root
- Salt
- Rosemary
- 1 capful to 1/4 cup ammonia

To bring the positive influences into your life:

- White flowers
- Honey
- Your favorite perfume
- Lavender

Make a strong infusion of first five ingredients. Use roughly equal parts of everything but the ammonia. Use up to 1/4 cup of the ammonia, as much as you can stand, and add to your bath. This will break up the negative influences. Then, add roughly equal amounts of the last four ingredients, except the perfume. Add that according to your own taste and preference. This will bring positive influences into your life.

Seven Day Frigga Cleansing Bath

This bath was given to me by Galina Krasskova. Frigga is the Goddess of the home in Norse Cosmology. She is incredibly powerful in Her own right and is not to be underestimated. Krasskova refers to Her as a Divine power-broker.

To make this bath, boil one cup each of the following ingredients for 20 minutes:

- Rosemary
- Fresh squeezed lime juice

- Basil
- Chamomile
- Cinnamon
- Lavender
- Rose petals or lemon verbena (I prefer the verbena)

Ask Frigga's blessing as you boil the herbs. Ask that She banish any negativity or harmful energies being sent your way. Add a cup of the resulting infusion to your bath for seven days in a row.

Generic Cleansing Bath

In two quarts of apple cider vinegar, add 2 tablespoons of each of the following ingredients:

- Lavender
- Rosemary
- Sage
- Wormwood
- Rue
- Mint

Add six mashed cloves of garlic and let it sit for 6 weeks in a cool, dark place. Then add a bit of crumbled camphor. This will keep for several months. When you wish to take a cleansing bath, strain out a cup and add it to your bathwater.

A Very Basic White Bath

Take seven white carnations and as you bathe, scrub yourself down with the flowers. This will cleanse your aura. If you can't find white carnations, it can be done with any bundle of white flowers or herbs. Be sure to discard the herbs afterward. They can be put right in the garbage, but I'd take them out immediately.

෨෨ Another Basic Cleansing Bath ෨෨

Make a strong infusion of the following herbs, all of which are either cleansing or useful in opening one's internal energy channels:

- ෨෨ Peppermint
- ෨෨ Rue
- ෨෨ Fennel
- ෨෨ Chervil
- ෨෨ Mugwort

Add the infusion to your bath, along with a cup of kosher or sea salt.

From these examples, I think the general idea is clear. The ingredients and possible combinations are virtually endless, but the desired result is the same. If you do nothing else, do not neglect weekly or, at the very least, monthly cleansing baths.

Elemental Cleansings

The traditional elements of Earth, Air, Fire, and Water can be very powerful energetic allies.[3] To some, they represent our eldest ancestors.[4] To others, they are powerful magical beings. And to yet others, they represent psycho-emotional-spiritual aspects of being—for example, Fire equals passion and creativity, Air equals intellect, Water equals emotion and psychic ability, and Earth equals strength and wealth. Regardless of how one approaches the elements, however, it is possible to call upon them for cleansings of people, places, and things.

Cleansing with Air

In traditional occultism, Air represents not only of the power of wind but also communication, the intellect, and an ability to make objective, rational decisions. Air cleansings usually involve smoke or incense. One may burn a cigar or cigarette and use the smoke to purify a room, an object, or even a person. Tobacco makes a fine offering to house spirits, ancestors, and even some Deities.

Burning *recels*, or bundles of herbs, to cleanse is a practice described in extant Anglo-Saxon medical manuals. (In those days, before industrialization and the national codification of medical standards, there was little difference between medicine and magic.[5]) This practice is called *smoking* or *smudging*. The bundle is ignited, and the fire blown out so that the herbs burn slowly, emitting smoke. The smoke is then passed around whomever or whatever needs to be cleaned. Crushed herbs and resins can be burned on small pieces of charcoal to achieve the same effect. Carrying this type of smoke throughout one's house is an excellent way to purify the dwelling. The same principles for creating cleansing baths apply to creating incenses. Combine herbs and resins for a specific purpose. Look in a good magical herbal (several are recommended at the end of this book) and choose herbs that are known to be effective for a particular purpose. Some of the best herbs and resins to use for cleansing and purification are as follows:

- Dragon's blood
- Sage
- Mugwort
- Frankincense
- Camphor
- Eucalyptus
- Hyssop

- Rosemary
- Copal
- Lemon balm
- Cedar
- Tobacco
- Garlic
- Asafetida (Warning: This is absolutely vile. Some people are highly sensitive to this herb so test it out before you burn it. I've known it to make some magicians vomit copiously. It is effective and quite powerful, however.)

For a **serious banishing incense**, mix equal parts agrimony, rue, and vervain, plus half a part of dragon's blood.

For two **good cleansing incenses**, mix equal parts sage, cinnamon, and rosemary; or frankincense, cinnamon, and brown sugar (good for bringing wealth into a dwelling).

For a **reasonably strong cleansing incense**, mix equal parts myrrh, white sandalwood, and cedar, and a half part dragon's blood powder.

For a **purification incense**, mix equal parts or thoroughly ground frankincense, white sandalwood, and copal.

For **my favorite cleansing and consecrating incense**, mix equal parts cedar and sage, and a half part tobacco.

One can also cleanse with sound, as it is associated magically with Air. Sound vibrations have the ability to break up stagnant energies. Using a rattle or, better yet, a Tibetan singing bowl in every room in your house with the intent of driving out negative or stagnant energy is a potent cleansing method. Be sure to have a window open when you clean a house magically—the energy needs somewhere to go.

Tuning forks can be used to clear negative energy out of stones. This is extremely efficient because it takes no personal energy nor does it require any innate psi- or magical talent. I use a tuning fork with the frequency of C 4096 to clear stones of any negative energy and one charged to 156.1 Herz to infuse them with earth energies. The spirits of the stones absolutely love this. Tuning forks can be purchased at *www.biosonics.com*.

I know of one magician who, before she moved into her new house, took a CD player and set it to repeat one CD over and over again. She then played the Heart Sutra for a solid 48 hours before moving in. She said it left her new home cleansed and blessed like nothing else she'd ever done. So don't underestimate the use of sound and music in ritual cleansings.

The element of Air is often symbolized by a blade in ritual work. You can also see this in tarot decks, in which the suit of swords represents the element. There are ways to cleanse with a sacred knife or sword. No matter what method you choose, however, the blade should always be kept in pristine condition, well-sharpened and well-oiled.[6] You can hold the knife or sword, feeling energy flowing from the earth through your hands and into the blade. Trace the person's (or your own) auric field with the blade. Do not really cut anyone. (There are ways of cleansing that involve ritual cutting, but they are beyond the scope of this book.) Outline the aura and think of cutting away anything negative, alien, or malignant.[7]

Cleansing with Fire

Fire by its very nature consecrates and purifies. In traditional occultism it is represented by the wand, because Fire is about projecting the will, and the wand is a representational tool of one's working will. Wands are usually crafted out of wood, which is fitting, as real fire often draws its life by consuming wood.

Fire will happily feed upon all types of energy. It has been used the world over in consecrating, blessing, and cleansing rituals. Carrying a candle or oil lamp around your home while asking Fire to cleanse and consecrate, to devour negative or stagnant energy, and to safely purify your home is an excellent method of cleansing. Better yet, bless and charge one candle for every room in your house. Charge each candle with the instructions to devour all negative energy as they burn, and allow them to burn all the way down. Remember that each of the elements is alive. They have their own type of sentience. They are deserving of respect. Furthermore, in many traditions, including my own Norse one, the elements are our eldest of ancestors. So be courteous and polite to them. This especially holds true with Fire.

Cleansing with Water

In addition to cleansing baths, which certainly fall under this category, there are several other ways to use water in this way. In addition to being cleansing, Water can also be extremely protective. It's easy to forget that water is tremendously powerful. It has an uncontrollable aspect to its nature that we, living as most of us do in safe, civilized environments, don't often get to witness. In traditional occultism, water is symbolized by a chalice and represents emotion and psychic ability.

A simple charm to protect you while you sleep is to put a glass of water by your bed. Throw it away every morning, clean the glass thoroughly, and don't use the glass for anything else. When we sleep and dream, we are sometimes vulnerable because we relax the guard we may have up during the day. If your home is fully warded, this isn't as important, but if you are traveling or if you have chosen not to thoroughly ward your home for some reason, this is a nice and simple protective measure. Sprinkling lavender water about your bed is also a nice way of ensuring good, clean energy. Special care should be taken with your bedroom, because dreams open you to the realms of potential manifestation.

Infusions of various herbs can also be sprinkled about your home to cleanse and alter its energy. A blend of marjoram and basil is particularly good for this. An infusion is made by boiling water and steeping the herbs in the water. The longer you steep the herbs, the stronger the infusion will be. Certain colognes, which can be purchased in botanicas, are also excellent for this purpose. My personal favorite is called Sandalo. This is also very effective at "cooling" a space down after magical or energetic workings. (Energy can translate very differently to people. Sometimes energy-work can make a room feel cold, sometimes warm or hot. When it goes too far in either extreme, it can be uncomfortable. Infusions and colognes are easy and effective methods of recreating balance.)

In addition to using water, many energy-workers, magicians, and healers also use stones and other accoutrements. These items can also collect diseased, stagnant, or negative energy as the practitioner works with them. They, too, need to be cleaned occasionally. Stones and other items can be cleansed by soaking them in salt water overnight. The water should then be flushed down the toilet. Some stones, such as amber or angelite, are fragile and porous, and salt will mar their beauty. Some tools might be damaged by submersion in salt water, too. In such cases, use an Air or Fire cleansing (pass the flame around the object).

Cleansing with Earth

Earth is the element of grounding and strength. On Wiccan and Pagan altars, it is usually symbolized by a pentacle, and on magical altars, by a pentacle or bowl of salt. Stones, evergreens, and soil are also used.

There are a number of ways this element can be called upon in cleansings. Crystals or other stones can be charged to collect negative or hostile incoming energy, and can then be placed at strategic points around the home. The downside with this is that they will need to be cleansed regularly. Items can be buried in the earth overnight for cleansing. Sand, soil, cascarilla powder, and even seeds can be charged to collect negative energy and then sprinkled over the floor of one's home. They are then swept up and out of the house. (Afterward, I usually sprinkle a calming infusion about the dwelling.) Stalks of plants such as mugwort and various types of white flowers can be used to actually rub a person down, thus cleansing them of negative energies. I've seen the same technique used to clean a home; the floors and walls are beaten with the plant or flower bundles, which are then discarded outside of the home.

Salt is a gift of the earth and is extraordinarily cleansing by itself. It may be sprinkled in a house and the vacuumed or swept up, added to baths, or sprinkled across the threshold. I also consider actual housecleaning to be a kind of earth-based cleansing, because it is a practice of honoring the corporeal, the physical, and the mundane.

A Quick Guide to
Energetically Cleansing a Home

The process of cleansing a home is very much the same as that of cleansing a person or an object. The combination of techniques is essentially the same. I recommend the following steps for a basic house cleansing:

1. Clean the house physically. This alone goes a long way toward preventing energetic nastiness. There's just nothing for the negative energy to latch onto.

2. Smudge with one of the cleansing herbs already mentioned.

3. Carry fire through each room, asking that Fire bless the space and remove any negative energy.

4. Asperse with an infusion of cleansing herbs.

5. Sprinkle salt over the threshold and the window sills.

Head Cleansings

In some traditions, most notably those of Afro-Caribbean cultures, practitioners believe that everyone has a guardian spirit of the head. This is essentially that part of our spirit that is always in connection with Deity—our higher self, if you will. In times of stress, exhaustion, or magical attack, it can be very helpful to "feed" this spirit by performing a head cleansing. It reopens the connection between this spirit and the Holy Powers.

I recommend doing a head cleansing at least once a year. I offer a traditional Santerian head cleansing as it was taught to me years ago, but as I am an eclectic magic-worker, I have also used various combinations of herbs and powders for this purpose with great effect. I offer one of my own combinations, as well, for comparison. Use your intuition here or seek out a qualified practitioner to prescribe a head cleansing. The process is rather messy, but it is very effective.

⬧ Head Cleansing #1 ⬧

Begin by giving an offering to Oshun, the Orisha of love, affection, fertility, and relationships. She likes honey, but you taste it first before offering it. (In one of Her sacred stories, someone tried to poison Her with this, her favorite food.) She also likes oranges, eggs, and gold. For this cleansing you will need equal amounts of the following ingredients:

- ๑๕ Coconut water
- ๑๕ River water or rain water
- ๑๕ Goat's milk
- ๑๕ Rice water (soak rice in a pot of water outside overnight)
- ๑๕ Cocoa butter
- ๑๕ Juice of "white" fruits such as pineapples, pears, honeydew melons, and sweet soursop

Mix these ingredients together and wash your head with them, purposefully offering the cleansing to the spirit of your head.

๑๕ Head Cleansing #2 ๑๕

Begin by making an offering to Freya. She likes honey, honey powder, Goldschläger, expensive chocolate, amber, gold, strawberries, and good quality perfume. For the offering, mix equal amounts of the following ingredients:

- ๑๕ Honey
- ๑๕ Crushed and powdered amber
- ๑๕ Damiana
- ๑๕ Rue
- ๑๕ Milk (preferably sweetened condensed milk)
- ๑๕ Goat's milk
- ๑๕ Cinnamon
- ๑๕ Ground coffee beans
- ๑๕ Shea butter

Wash your head with this mixture, offering it to the spirit of your head. This is not a traditional practice within the Northern Tradition, but it is still effective.

Magical Oils

There are numerous recipes on the market for magical oils, so I'm only going to offer a few of my own recipes here. Oils can be used for blessing and consecrating; to mark one's ownership of an object; and to draw protective sigils on people, places, and things. Although one of the clearest and most powerful ways to mark ownership of an object or mark a person as under your own protection is to use your own blood, this isn't always appropriate. Even if you are in a "fluid bond" with someone, there are obvious health concerns. Also, blood also creates the single strongest connection you can possibly have with an object; if that object is lost or falls into the wrong hands, the results can be most unpleasant. So, all in all, it's better not to use blood—hence the proliferation of magical oils. Most oils are mixed by adding a certain number of drops to a carrier oil. I prefer to use sweet almond oil as the carrier.

✨ Power and Protection Oil ✨

- ✨ 1 small chuck of jalap
- ✨ 2 parts dragon's blood oil
- ✨ 1 part frankincense oil
- ✨ 1/2 part poke root
- ✨ 1/2 part galangal root or oil

Mix into a base oil of sweet almond oil, and store with a piece of carnelian.

ೞ Power Oil ೞ

Mix equal parts frankincense, myrrh, and dragon's blood oils. This oil works as an incense, too, if the required resins are used.

ೞ Blessing Oil #1 ೞ

Mix 1 part wisteria, 1 part rose, and 1/2 part lavender oils.

ೞ Blessing Oil #2 ೞ

Mix equal parts benzoin, wisteria oil, and lilac oil.

ೞ Purification Oil ೞ

Mix 1 part camphor, 1/2 part musk, 1/2 part rose oil, and a touch of patchouli oil.

Cleansing for Diviners

Divination is the art of reading fate, luck, and the future through a medium such as the tarot, runes, the I-Ching, lithomancy, or scrying. Usually it requires some degree of precognition. Because effective divination often requires the reader to put him- or herself into a receptive state of mind, common sense dictates a certain amount of preparation and after-cleansing.

I suggest thoroughly smudging the room in which you will conduct the reading with cleansing and protective herbs. If possible, take a cleansing bath before the client arrives. I usually wear a protective amulet during the divination, because effectively reading for the client means "thinning out" my regular personal shields for the duration of the reading. Because

I am a magician, I usually perform the LBP (Lesser Banishing Pentagram) before the client arrives, as well. It's also good to make small offerings to your house spirits and ancestors, asking them to keep a protective eye on you during the reading and ward off any negative influences. Many diviners I know who are also deeply religious offer prayers to the Deity or Deities of their choice prior to a reading. Before the client arrives, I also suggest 10 or 15 minutes of grounding and centering, unless this is something that makes it more difficult for you to enter into the light trance usually required for divination.[8]

After the reading, the diviner remains in a vulnerable position for some time. Divination can occasionally attract ancestral and other spirits, which will hover about the person being read. These spirits have their own agendas, and the reader can sometimes find him- or herself being influenced by them even after the reading has ended. For this reason, it's important to know yourself, know how you think, and know how your thoughts feel and sound in your own head. Self-knowledge is the key. Right after a reading, if you suddenly find yourself aching to do something that is completely out of character, or thinking unusual thoughts that don't seem to be in alignment with your usual self, it may be a sign that a spirit is trying to influence you. It is also possible to pick up negative energy from the querent (the person being read), and this can affect your health, energy, and emotions.

For this reason, I recommend cleansing the reading space immediately after the client leaves. I usually asperse with a cleansing infusion and break up any negative energy using sound. Drums, rattles, and Tibetan bowls all work well for this. I may also choose to smudge with a protective and cleansing herb such as mugwort. Additionally, because Fire is one of my primary allies, I often leave a candle burning during a reading. I light it before the client arrives, asking the spirits of Fire to devour any negative energy that the client may leave in my space. If I feel any sense of unease, I place camphor squares in the four corners of the room and set out a cup of red vinegar to block and ward off negative spirit manifestation, respectively. Finally, I change my clothes immediately after a reading; if I have the time, I also take a cleansing bath.

The most important thing is to be mindful that the receptivity necessary in divining may render you vulnerable to spirit influence or negative energy from the querent. That mindfulness will be your best guide to effective action.

6

Basic Energy-Work and Magic

*Excellence is an art won by training and habituation.
We do not act rightly because we have virtue or
excellence, but we rather have those because we have
acted rightly. We are what we repeatedly do.
Excellence, then, is not an act but a habit.*

—*Aristotle*

Sometimes there is a very fine line between energy-work and magic. In many respects, they're two sides of the same esoteric coin. Energy-work, as I have already stated, involves tapping into natural energies and becoming a conduit for them. Usually the goal is cleansing, energetic balancing, or some type of healing. Magic involves the same tapping and appropriation of natural energies, but it is more clearly defined as the craft of using energy directly through the conduits of the will and the body to affect circumstances in a clearly defined and predictable manner. In this case there is much more emphasis on active manifestation of the will in attaining a specific goal. It is not the "art of changing consciousness at will," as some contemporary practitioners assert. That describes a useful technique, but it is not magic per se. Nor is it prayer, as many Neo-Pagans believe. Magic is about the purposeful application of raw power, and anyone who tells you differently doesn't know much about magic. For all practical purposes, at least for this book, many of the same truisms still hold true, whether one is talking about generic energy-work or magic. Basically, anything that involves the purposeful manipulation of energy is magic. If they differ at all, it's a difference in focus and application more than anything else.

All of the props and tools mentioned in this and many other books on the subject are, in reality, tangential to actual practice. They are tools to help focus the will, but they are not in and of themselves necessary. There's the old axiom repeated by many teachers of the Art that one should be able to work magic effectively in the nude, in an empty room at 4 a.m. and with absolutely no props, and that axiom holds true for both magic and energy-work. The only necessary tools—will and focus—are within oneself. To do anything with energy effectively, two things are needed: a sensitivity to energy and a disciplined will. With magic, a high tolerance to pain and discomfort doesn't hurt either.

The aforementioned sensitivity is an inborn gift, just as the psi-talents mentioned in Chapter 3 are. It enables one to sense or see energy currents and to pull them up so that they can be used.[1] Energy-work is a very individual practice in that everyone finds their own way. Energy can translate to people in many different ways. Some people have the facility to see or feel it. Others may experience it as colors, changes in temperature, different smells, even changes in one's emotional and physical balance. It's important to develop an awareness of how external energy translates to you individually. Know your own responses. Don't worry overmuch if the way you perceive and interact with it differs from other practitioners.

It's been my experience that people with strong psi-talents usually have at least a little talent for working magic or doing energy-work—certainly enough to do the various exercises in this book. This facility can usually be developed by honing one's concentration and disciplining one's will. In addition to a daily regimen of centering and grounding, there are dozens of ways that one can perform the most mundane tasks with magical intent, inculcating those tasks with the goal of training. This can help whether one wishes to advance to magic or merely develop skills as a generic energy-worker. The initial training regimen is largely the same for both.

For instance, if you tend to procrastinate, don't allow yourself to indulge this tendency. Nip it in the bud; do not allow it to flower. Change your inborn tendencies and habitual behavior by purposeful and repeated application of your will. If you are prone to outbursts of temper, rein it in. When you next want to bite the head off of the retail clerk who has annoyed you, curb that impulse and instead be icily polite. It won't kill you and such things go a long way toward developing the will. To be truly competent in both energy-work and magic, it's not enough to have the gift for sensing and working with energy; the most essential tool is a strongly disciplined will. Basically, if you cannot control your own passions, you cannot effectively or safely practice magic.

Learn to curb your appetites, too. Make it a habit to fast one day a week. If you have a medical condition that precludes this, limit your food intake to a bit of fruit and grains for the day, and drink only water. This helps to subordinate the desires to the will. There is a classical Roman saying that if one cannot fast for a one day out of the week, one has no right to call oneself an adult. Desire is good, but only when it is not one's master.

This brings up an important point. The majority of negative energy sent your way, up to and including a full-blown attack, is probably not being sent by trained magicians or energy-workers. People can send negative energy without even realizing it. Energy will go where will, attention, and intent go. If someone is angry or jealous, or if they really dislike someone, and they actively focus on this feeling with a sudden burst of emotion, that energy can involuntarily be directed toward a victim. This is the origin of *malocchio*, or the evil eye. Most people don't realize that their emotions have the power to harm in this way. After all, emotion is energy. You will notice that I have not included any techniques for either binding or hexing an opponent in this book. This is largely because it takes more than book knowledge to ferret out whether an attack is intentional or not. It also takes more than book knowledge to be able to bind or counterattack safely and effectively. The techniques given here will disperse pretty much anything other than a well-planned attack by a trained and highly skilled magician (and quite possibly some of that, as well). For the rest, there is no shame in calling in outside help.

Another facet of magic and energy-work to consider is that as much as they are metaphysical experiences, they are also physical ones. When you work with energy your body becomes a conduit for the energies involved. This can create a tremendous physical and even emotional and/or psychological strain. Do what you can to offset that by keeping yourself healthy and in good physical shape. Exercise, eat right, and get enough sleep—admittedly all easier said than done. Getting regular and sufficient sleep is particularly important as it gives the brain time to rest and recharge. If I had to choose between eating and sleeping, sleep would win every time. Sleeping regularly, even more so than eating, is the first step in preventing any imbalance.

Studying a martial art, for both the physical discipline and the sensitivity to energy that it brings, is an excellent idea, as is the study of qi gong. Meditating for 10 or 15 minutes a day in a comfortable position, using the relaxation exercises given in Chapter 1, is also very helpful. That said, there are a few other basic exercises that will enable one to learn to sense energy more easily and actively manipulate that energy.

Raising Energy

This is the most basic exercise in energy manipulation. In order to do anything with energy, you have to learn how to tap into it and actually raise it with your will and your mental "hands." Begin by centering and grounding strongly. Extend your senses into the earth and feel for a line of energy. When you feel a little jolt, draw the energy into you through your "inbound" grounding channel and allow it to flow into your hands. Your hands may tingle, and you may feel a certain warmth. Either use the energy for something or send it back down through your "outbound" grounding channel. If you cannot sense it, see it, or feel it, that's okay. Use your imagination and visualize it as best you can. Sometimes this is the first key to unlocking ability. Without a teacher, it can often feel as though you are fumbling around in the dark. Only ongoing and dogged practice can change this. The basic grounding and centering exercises, when done with the visualizations given in Chapter 1, will help you develop your capacity for sensing and interacting with energy. The extended chakra exercise is particularly effective.

Shaping Energy

After you've learned how to draw energy up, the next exercise is learning how to shape it into something. The most common technique is the creation of energy balls. Draw energy up and into your hands. Feel and see it glowing there. Shape it with your will and mind into a sphere. Once you've gotten the hang of this, try making the sphere bigger by feeding more energy into it, or smaller by taking energy away. To make it stronger, feed more energy into it; to weaken it, ground some energy out of it. Once you've gained confidence with this exercise, try doing it with a friend. Feel the energy flowing into your hands and then push and pull the energy back and forth between you. Feel free to experiment and play. This is how you will gain both skill and confidence.

Charging Objects

Next, once you've confidently mastered making energy balls, try charging something. Take a coin or a stone and charge the hell out of it. This means raising energy and, instead of playing with it, sending it into the object in question. Seal it in by cleanly severing any connection the energy may have to you. Do this by tying it off into the object and visualizing a clean separation between you and it. Some energy-workers may wish to draw a sacred symbol of their choice over the object with their fingers. Then, place the stone or coin amongst several other similar stones or coins and leave it there for a few hours. Come back to it and see if you can tell by feel which is the charged object. Basic candle magic is an excellent means of learning how to charge objects. It's also nice in that it's a simple form of energy-work which, if properly focused, can yield immed⋅ results.

Using Blood

Blood is the most potent substance you will ever work with. It creates one of the strongest links possible. This applies whether you are using it to create a link to a person or whether you are using your own blood to bind a tool to your hand alone. It is a powerful substance. If you choose to use blood in energy-work or magic (and some allies will require it; the runes certainly do on a regular basis), the most potent blood is that drawn by your own hand with intent. As I stated in the previous chapter, menstrual blood is, for the most part, utterly useless in magic. It is waste blood. It has some uses in hoodoo love charms and can occasionally be used in fertility magic, but beyond that, it's a weak substance. Better not to use blood at all than to use what is effectively a second-rate substance. If you don't have the will to draw blood with a tool, you don't have the will to work the spell.[2]

The best way to draw blood is with a diabetic lancet. These can be purchased in bulk at most pharmacies. Be sure to clean the puncture afterward. Each lancet should be used only once and then disposed of. I put my used lancets in a "sharps" container, which I then dispose of when it's full. Sharps containers can usually be dropped off at drug stores or your doctor's office. Medically speaking, blood is a dangerous substance. Don't ever share implements with anyone.

Keep in mind that using blood in a charm creates a connection that could be used against you should the charm ever fall into the wrong hands. Guard your blood as you would guard your own life, and never, ever give it to another magician. That goes for menstrual blood, as well, for although it isn't as potent as blood that has been purposefully drawn for a spell, it still comes from you and thus can create a magical link. Just be cautious and don't allow anything from your person—blood, sexual fluids,

hair, nail clippings, even clothing—to fall into someone else's
hands.

Wyrd

As I have already noted, the way I practice both energy-
work and magic is largely informed by my religious practices
and the Norse cosmology in which I work. Within Norse cosmology there is something called Wyrd. Wyrd is causality and
consequence. It's inherited luck and obligation along with our
own actions, choices, successes, and failures. Wyrd is created
by the sum total of our actions and choices, combined with
those of our ancestors, which we inherit. It is a powerful force
in and of itself and should not be underestimated or treated
disrespectfully.[3] We can shape our Wyrd to some degree, making it stronger or weaker by the choices we make and how we
behave. Wyrd is so powerful that even the Gods must obey
it. This force is usually seen as a vast, complex web stretching
farther than the eye can see. It's similar to a layered maze of ley
lines that can be felt, read, and sometimes actively manipulat-
ed. Every single person has their own personal thread of Wyrd,
which is called *orlog*.

Because Wyrd connects all living things, and because it
forms the fabric out of which the world is made, it's possible to
navigate it. Reading the threads of Wyrd and what they contain is called *spae*. Working it directly, altering its flow and
reweaving the threads, is a form of magic. It is through careful
examination of the threads that one can determine what can
lawfully be cast, and how best to cast for good effect. It is also
possible to read the consequences and possible repercussions of
what one is casting.

Magical Tools

I want to say a few words about magical tools. Both magicians and energy-workers have an notable tendency to collect pretty tools. All of us go through a phase in which we want the newest, biggest, shiniest things to use in our practice. This is normal. Tools can enhance the practice of energy-work and magic because they give us something tactile and concrete to hold onto. They provide a physical focus. But that is all they do, so one shouldn't break the bank trying to acquire a vast array of stones, oils, animal skins, knives, crystals, and so on. It's really not necessary.

Certain tools are mentioned time and time and again—namely, the knife, wand, chalice, and pentacle. These are generally associated with Wicca but they can actually trace their origins back to the Renaissance and, later, to ceremonial magic. We see them represented in the minor arcana of the tarot along with their elemental representations: Air, Fire, Water, and Earth, respectively. Magicians work with these four classical elements.[4] Each element has a magical tool associated with it. These tools occasionally come in handy in magical workings, including protection work, so I'm going to touch on them briefly here. However, with the exception of the knife, they do not figure greatly in my own work.

The tool of Air: the knife

Magically, Air is usually associated with the intellect, with the power of decision-making, with clarity, with purification, with cleansing, and with cutting away that which is no longer needed. It represents intellectual pursuits, fluency in/facility with language (including the ability to cut someone to ribbons with words), and the power of speech as magical manifestation. The negative traits associated with this element are flightiness, a lack of focus, and a certain vapidity. Those who have a particular affinity for Air and wind often struggle with the inherent power of language, with the knowledge that words, like arrows once loosed, can never be called back. That is the particular lesson of this element. It teaches the need for focus and mindfulness. Traditionally, the direction of this element is east, its colors are blue and white or yellow (depending on which ceremonial tradition one practices), and its tool is the knife.

Of all the tools I own, the only one I use regularly is my knife, or *athame*. It is an all-purpose tool, consecrated and blessed, fully charged and ready to be used in combat or for such practical purposes as cutting bread or thread. Please keep your knife in good working order—clean, oiled, and sharpened at all times. I absolutely deplore the fallacy that has circulated in Pagan, Wiccan, and some magical circles for years that one's working blade should be dull. This is an utter disgrace—to the magic, to the spirit of the blade itself, to the weapon, to the blade-smith, and to every single one of your ancestors who had to use a blade for survival. This idea that blades should be dulled, that the edge should be purposefully blunted is, to be quite blunt, a load of New Age bullshit.

Please do not purchase a decorative blade. Purchase a real knife, one that could stand up to a bit of hard work. Either go to a sporting goods store and check out their selection of blades, or find a good online dealer: *www.ragweedforge.com*, *www.knifeworks.com*, or *www.coldsteel.com* are all excellent online shops with extensive and well-priced catalogs. Learn how to care for your knife, including how to properly sharpen it. I prefer to have one fixed blade for fighting and magical purposes, and one folding blade for utilitarian purposes, but this is purely a personal preference. A good blade is a multipurpose tool. Blades should not be cleaned energetically with salt water. It is best to clean them with sacred smoke. Be sure to oil the blade appropriately after cleaning, and wipe off any excess oil before storing it in its sheath.

If you have the means, you should learn how to use your blade. This includes knife fighting. I recommend martial arts training to every would-be magician and energy-worker. Not only does it teach fighting skills (which are always useful in this day and age), but it also helps instill discipline, grounds you in your own skin, and can teach you a thing or two about the flow of energy in the body.

Blades are very useful in consecrating a space. Power can be drawn up and channeled through the blade. Moreover, having a blade on one's altar or in one's kit of tools is a visual reminder of the need for objectivity, focus, and careful mindfulness. It reminds us that survival sometimes means struggle, and that our ancestors often had to make difficult decisions in order to thrive. It is also a symbol of the warrior's will and of the responsibilities that come with power.

Such knives can also be used to cut etheric cords. This is an important function. Whenever we interact with someone on a physically intimate level (particularly during sex or energy-work), connections of energy, magic, and intent are formed. These etheric cords ensure that energy is shared between two people, and they tie the two together, magically and spiritually, unless they are cut. It is very easy for a magician to influence another person through these connections. This is the reason why so many traditional spells call for something personal belonging to the intended victim: a picture, nail clippings, hair, semen, blood, or even a piece of clothing.

If someone is under magical attack, sometimes it is because someone else is using one of these cords (regardless of how it was formed) as a link to the victim. In cases such as this, it is necessary to cut the cord, which can occasionally be somewhat unpleasant. People with the gift of sight can actually see cords, but if someone with that particular talent isn't available, it's often possible to use your own intuition to ferret out where the cord is connecting. Usually they connect at the root, sex, or solar plexus chakra.

To cut a cord, first locate it. Then take the blade in your hands, draw energy up, and channel it into the blade. Cut the cord (not the person!) just as you would a piece of rope or string. Then seal the person by marking a protective rune such as Algiz over the spot where the cord was cut. You might also carry fire around the person's aura to seal it off from such outside influence in the future. This is the energetic equivalent of cauterizing a wound. Do not actually burn the person.

The tool of Fire: the wand

The element of Fire is usually associated with the will, strength, courage, passion, creativity, vibrancy, transformation, and destruction. The negative traits associated with this element are anger and a lack of control over one's passions. It teaches the need for discipline—of oneself, of one's hungers, of one's passions, of one's desires. Traditionally, the direction of this element is south, its colors are vibrant red and orange, and its tool is the wand. It is symbolically significant that the tool for this element is traditionally crafted out of wood, the fuel on which fire usually feeds. This reminds us that without discipline, everything we seek to create and craft can be destroyed by our own lack of self-regulation. One lapse of control, one slip of the necessary discipline, one yielding to anger's song, and one's reputation, relationships, and work can all be marred or forever destroyed. Fire devours wood, but we must be the ones who control when to feed fuel to our own inner fire.

When I was training, I was required to make my own wand. I chose the wood very carefully (for its magical purposes), sanded it down, wood-burned the appropriate sigils on it (in my case runes) affixed a stone at the bottom and a pointed crystal at the tip, binding them with copper wire and adding decorative leather. It was a potent meditation. Admittedly though, I usually use the knife for anything that a more traditional magician would utilize the wand for. If you feel the need to make a wand, know that it represents fire and is used to stir up and direct magical energy. In some ceremonial traditions, the knife is the tool of Fire and the wand of Air (which makes more sense to me actually, as the wand is used to direct energy) but this is definitely a minority opinion.

The tool of Water: the chalice

The element of Water is usually associated with psychic ability, emotions, magic, intuition, and dreaming. The negative traits associated with this element are indecisiveness and excessive emotionality. This element reminds us that emotional responses don't always represent truth, and that while our feelings may be beyond our control, we need not allow them to dictate our actions. It also reminds us to be flexible in all things, to guard against becoming rigid and hidebound. Traditionally, the direction of this element is west, its color is deep blue, and its tool is the chalice.

I've never understood why Water is so often dismissed as a weak element. It's anything but. Water is arguably the strongest element of the four. It's incredibly flexible: it can remain in liquid form, turn into steam, or transform into ice and yet it maintains its essential nature. It can be every bit as destructive and vicious as Fire—just witness the destruction of a tsunami or a hurricane. In fact, some people work with Ice as a completely separate element. The attributions I've given here are the traditional ceremonial magic attributions. Norse cosmology would assign far different roles to Water, for in that world-matrix, the universe was created through a conflagration of Ice and Fire. It's a toss-up as to which was/is the dominant element.

A chalice filled with water is usually used to represent this element. I've found this to be surprisingly useful during workings; magically speaking, having the four tools and elements present reminds me of their power and how this power can be properly used in a working. It's a reminder to be respectful and to seek balance in these things. You could fill a chalice with ice, charge that ice with a specific intent, and then allow it to melt, using the act of melting as the release mechanism for the spell. Ice is all about transformation, but on a radically different level from that of Fire. In both cases, there is change and destruction, and a new creation that comes about through the inherent change within the element. Ice is the most hierarchical of elements. Working with Ice will teach you, above all else, to know your place. This is not a bad thing. There is little judgment attached to the concept of one's rightful place. It is a matter of knowing your place and thereby knowing where you will be most effective and efficient. Ice is about power.[5]

Using a chalice or bowl to hold whatever infusions you're making to cleanse your home is a good idea, too. If you use a tool repeatedly for magic or energy-work, it picks up a special charge. It becomes empowered, and this power can assist in charging whatever it holds. Personally, I think this is the real reason that the use of these tools is so widespread. Magicians tend to be territorial and that extends to investing their tools with a certain amount of power. The charge that an oft-used tool can acquire can make the outcome of a particular working yours. There's also the practical to consider. For instance, after

I've gone through the trouble of consecrating and charging a knife or a bowl, why would I want to repeat that? It makes more pragmatic sense just to use the same bowl or knife over and over again. I've occasionally used a mortar and pestle to represent both Earth and Water, but this wouldn't be considered a traditional approach.

The tool of Earth: the pentacle

The element of Earth is usually associated with healing, fertility, strength, growth, and the ancestors. The negative traits associated with this element are excessive sensuality, avarice, and procrastination. This elements reminds us to strive for balance, to govern our desires without either denying or overindulging them. Earth is all about being properly grounded and doing things in the proper time and manner. It's about understanding both tradition and innovation, and finding an organic balance of both. It's also about wise financial management and management of one's resources. Traditionally, the direction of this element is north, its colors are vibrant green and brown, and its tool is the pentacle, which also symbolizes the balanced union of all four classical elements with Spirit.

When I feel the need to have all four elements represented on my working altar, I usually prefer to use either a bowl of salt, a bowl of soil, a bit of evergreen, or a crystal or some other type of stone to represent Earth. This is because the pentacle has become so strongly associated with Wicca, becoming in effect its sacred symbol. This is not out of any disrespect for Wicca as a religion; rather, it is because I personally am uncomfortable in appropriating a sacred symbol that has become so very strongly associated with a particular religion. I'm all for using whatever works, but there are a few areas where I draw the line. For the same reason, I wouldn't use a Star of David in workings on my altar, though it has a history in ceremonial magic.

The tool of the Spirit: the altar

There really is no particular tool commonly used to represent Spirit or ether. Throughout the years, and under the influence of my own teachers, I've come to see the altar itself as that symbol. I'm of the opinion that everyone should have an altar. Spiritually, it's a wonderful way to honor the Gods and can be a nice focal point for prayers and offerings. From the perspective of a magician, it's a practical place to actively manifest one's spells and rituals. From a traditional standpoint, it's a powerful symbol of spiritual focus, balance, and commitment. Those familiar with tarot will note that the traditional representations of the magician card in the major arcana show an altar prominently displayed. It is the foundation on which the other tools symbolically and literally rest.

For the magician, it's a good place to keep his or her tools and to perform the workings that require those tools. I prefer to use a smaller table as my work table. This is separate from my religious altar because its purpose is completely different. I keep my altar reasonably clean, and I cleanse it magically on a regular basis. This is where I will set up long-term charms. It's where I set my tools to charge. It's also where I work candle magic. Altars can be in any size, shape, and color. The important thing is that you have a place to work. You may never want or need any of these tools, but in the event that you do, you have the basic correspondences available here.

Casting a Circle

I'm loath to touch on this topic, but as much as I hate to admit it, it does have certain useful properties. Wicca uses this technique before every ritual to consecrate space. Ceremonial magic, from which Wicca originally co-opted the rite, uses it almost as often. Personally I don't see the need. If you want to work magic, sit down and do so. If you feel the need to ward your space, then work in your own warded house. Casting a circle in a ritual is a nice way to psychologically signify that one is moving out of normal space and into ritual space, but its uses in magic are far more restricted. Energy-workers and healers may choose to do it or not. I would suggest experimenting and seeing if you like the way it feels, if it enhances your practices or not. This is one of those aspects of practice that is really a matter of personal preference.

A magical circle is indeed used to ward space, but it's used to ward a specific and restricted space. I would use a circle:

- If I wanted to contain something.
- If I needed to put people or things in a protected space while I worked outside of that space.
- If I had to work magic in a completely unwarded and alien space.
- If I were engaged in some type of summoning ritual (which, as a general rule, I do not recommend).

Again, I emphasize pragmatism and efficiency. This is why I'm an eclectic, despite being fully trained in two different systems. As the saying goes, your mileage may vary. If you really feel the need to cast a circle every single time you work, go for it. To my mind, though, it's a waste of energy better spent elsewhere.

How to cast a circle

I am not going to discuss the myriad of ways one can do this in a ritual setting, be that ritual magical or religious. I'm also not going to discuss the "dog and pony show" of a full ceremonial rite, as this is not a book about ceremonial magic.

There are plenty of books that deal with that already anyway. I'm going to focus on the very narrow magical usage described previously. There are three quick ways to cast a circle:

- ✐ When you need to ward something, draw the circle out with chalk and verbally call forth power, channeling it into this act and saying something along the lines of, "I consecrate this circle of power that it may bind and protect, keeping out all that would do harm. So mote it be."

- ✐ Sprinkle salt around the object or person you wish to ward. (Salt has protective and purifying properties.)

- ✐ Take your blade or wand, center, draw power up, and channel it through the tool, walking in a clockwise circle around the space while verbally consecrating it.

These are my three quick-fix ways of casting a circle. When the work is over, the energy should be broken by either tracing over it clockwise with knife or wand, or consciously dispersing it and grounding it into the earth. It is extremely rare that I would need any more ritual than that.

Quick-fix protection rite

This is an incredibly efficient personal ward or quick-fix protection rite that I learned from my ceremonialist teacher. It is based on a medieval prayer (apparently my teacher found it quoted in a novel, though she could not recall the title of the book). It was something she had copied into her own magical journal and, because it was efficient, she taught it to me. I recommend it to both magicians and energy-workers. It is especially effective for the latter. If anyone knows where this was first used, I would love to have the original source. Note that this rite does not provide long-lasting protection. I wouldn't depend on it for more than 20 minutes, but that is ample time to cleanse a house or a person. This is a nice protection ritual to do before going into a situation in which you know you will be dealing with tainted, dangerous, or malignant energy. However, it is no substitute for good shields or for cleansing work after the fact.

1. Stand and center yourself. Perform the Kabbalistic cross.

2. Extend your arms to the side and say with focused intent: "By the power of the Gods within me, whom I serve with all my heart, with all my soul, and with all my breath."

3. Begin turning in a clock-wise circle, saying: "I now encompass myself about in this circle of Divine protection across which no mortal or immortal error dares to set its foot."

4. Perform the Kabbalistic cross again to close the rite.

Basic Candle Magic

Candle magic is a very good method of learning how to feel and manipulate energy. It is one of the most basic forms of practical magic, as well as one of the easiest. It's very elemental and simple to practice. Even if one has no desire to become a magician, this is an excellent (and enjoyable) way to learn to sense and manipulate energy. Energy-workers can benefit from this just as well as those seeking to gain occult mastery. There are generally four steps to the process of working a candle:

1. Cleansing
2. Charging
3. Etching
4. Sealing

Cleansing the candle

Because candles are often handled by several people and pick up various energies in their travels, it's good to do a quick and simple cleansing before you set it to your own purpose. I suggest smudging the candle with a purifying herb.

When I was a novice, I was instructed to dedicate the candle by saying something like, "I cleanse, bless, and purify this creature of wax for the magic at hand. This creature of wax is cleansed and purified, so mote it be." You can say this if you want, but why waste words? Do the four steps properly and this silly phrase is unnecessary. I've found a tendency in many magicians to invest themselves and their workings with a certain degree of self-importance. This is a tendency that one should work hard to break. Hubris is deadly to any magician or energy-worker. The gifts and skills that we acquire should be approached with humility. We may seek to act with power, but we are not Gods. Nor do these skills make us any better than anyone else. I try to shy away from anything that doesn't enhance the work but only serves my ego. Unwarranted arrogance is a demon against which every magician and energy-worker must fight an ongoing battle.

Charging the candle

All magic is based on will and intent, so keep this in mind as you set about charging the candle to the purpose you have chosen. Again, I was originally told to say, "Blessed be this creature of power, you are no more creature of wax, but creature of flesh and blood, and you know full well why and for whom you live," or "Blessed be this creature of magic; this creature of magic is fully alive, alive with purpose. This creature of magic knows well why and for whom it burns." Again, if you feel the need, go ahead and say something like this, but I find holding the purpose in my mind and filling the candle with energy works even better.

Ground yourself, feeling your connection to the earth as strongly as possible. Draw energy up and feel it flowing through your body, into your hands, and into the candle. Try to avoid using your internal energies, otherwise the power source is very limited. Once you master this drawing up and focusing of energy into the candle itself, it may actually shake in your hands, your hands may get hot, or the candle may melt a bit or feel heavier. Continue sending energy into it as you set that energy to the purpose you have chosen. (This is done by focusing intently on what you want and feeling the energy take on the shape and texture of that desire. Essentially, you're "imprinting" the energy with that desire.)

Etching the candle

Once you feel you have enough energy in the candle, seal it in by drawing an invoking pentacle with your fingers or a knife. Start at the point, move to lower left corner, up to the upper right corner, across to the upper left corner, down to the lower right corner, up to point, and then a clockwise circle. At this point, you may also want to carve onto the candle certain sigils, runes, or symbols to add more power. You can use a knife, a pin, a nail—whatever works best. It's always a good idea to also carve the name and astrological sign of the person for whom the spell is being performed. This helps to further focus the energy. Candles that cannot be removed from the jar can be empowered in the same way; just do the carving and oiling on the very top, and use a marker to draw whatever symbols you wish on the glass. Keep the intent fully in mind as you carve or draw. If you're using a seven-day candle (the kind that pulls out of the glass) and you want to get extra fancy, here are a few traditional items you can add:

- Iron filings in the bottom of the glass to draw down energy.
- Honey for love and prosperity spells.
- Dragon's blood for protection or combat magic.
- Incense or finely ground herbs to match the purpose of the magic.
- Pennies for wealth and manifestation.
- Oils to match the purpose of the magic.

According to tradition, someone tried to kill Ochun by giving her honey that had been poisoned, so if you use honey in your candle magic, be sure to taste it first. Some people light a spoonful of incense, dump it in the bottom of the jar, and then cover it so that the jar fills with smoke. Be creative.

Once you've charged and carved the candle, choose an oil that matches the purpose of the casting, pour some into your hand, and rub it all over the candle. If you wish, you may say, "With this oil and by and through these hands, I now empower this creature of magic to bring forth and manifest that which I desire, that which I will." As you rub the oil into the candle, keep your intent in mind. This is also a good time to add more energy. Unless the candle ignites in your hand, you haven't yet added too much energy.

Sealing the candle

Pick a resin or a ground or powdered herb—I usually use dragon's blood—and rub it into the carving. (Don't worry if the heat of your hands melts it somewhat.) This will highlight the carving. I use dragon's blood because it augments almost any magic and can draw powerful energy. It does make a mess, though, and doesn't wash off your hands very easily. If you wish to say something, try this: "This spell cannot be changed or altered by anyone or anything in any way or any manner. As is my will, so mote it be." This seals the charm. At this point, make another invoking pentacle and clap your hands to shake off any excess energy. This will sever any cords that link you to the magic. Envision the ties breaking as you clap your hands.

Finally, light the candle with intent. If you can't leave it burning, it's fine to blow it out as long as you re-light it with the same level of intent as the first time. I've known practitioners to put their candles in a container of water, so that if the glass surrounding the candle breaks, the water will flow in and put out the flame. Use your best judgment in this, as you should in all your workings.

When you are working any type of magic, have one and only one clear purpose in mind. Working magic is rather like giving instructions to a 4-year-old, so keep it very focused and very simple.

Types of candles

Go into the average occult shop and you'll see candles of all shapes, sizes, and colors for sale. Although it doesn't really matter in the long run what candle you use (I buy mine at the local grocery), the shape and color *can* help to focus the practitioner's will and energy, which can only strengthen the spell being worked. The size of the candle doesn't matter at all. It's the intent with which it is used, empowered, and lit. It's all about will. In other words, it's all in how you use it. Here are a few different kinds of candles and what they are typically used for:

- Skull candles: white is for uncrossing, healing, and clarity; black absorbs negativity; red is for love spells or to "get inside someone's head."

- Man/woman figurine candles: for sympathetic magic (love and healings).

- Black cat candles: for uncrossing.

- Cross candles: for psychic work, protection, uncrossing.

- Seven-knobbed candles: one knob is burned each day while the practitioner focuses intently on his/ her purpose.

- Penis/vagina candles: for sex magic, fertility, love, lust. Also used to represent the Gods and Goddesses.

- Witch candles: for good luck.

- Seven African Powers candles: for prayer, devotion, and uncrossing.[6]

Any candle may be used for devotional purposes; charge it with energy as a gift or simply light it. Candle magic in general is particularly good for healing work.

Colors

People can respond very powerfully to certain colors. They can be used to affect both mood and energy levels. Books have been written about the use of color in the workplace and the effect it can have on employees, and about the use of color as a healing tool. The same holds true in energy-work and magic, especially candle magic. Color can influence intent and emotions. If you're in doubt as to what color to choose, choose white. Again, color doesn't really matter as long as your intent is strong. The colors simply help you focus your intent. If you have a negative response to a certain color, it's best not to use it. Here are some common candle colors along with some associations and correspondences:

- Black: absorbs energy, used in retribution–type spells. May also be used in certain uncrossings and *warfetters* (bindings). Its planetary correspondence is Saturn.

- Brown: grounding, earth work. Its planetary correspondence is Earth, though I prefer to use this color for Saturn. It is excellent for healing charms, particularly for rebalancing one's energies.

- Purple: psychic development, crown chakra work, expansion, wealth, wisdom. Its planetary correspondence is Jupiter.

- Blue: calming, protection, peace, blessing, healing. Associated with water, fertility, psychic matters. Its planetary correspondences are Neptune and the moon.

- Green: money, earth, fertility, abundance, harvest, healing, removing stress. Its planetary correspondence is the earth.

- Yellow: healing, especially respiratory distress. Associated with the sun, energy-work, inspiration, creativity, success, and fame. Its planetary correspondence is the sun.

- Orange: success, opening things up, uncrossing, clarity, knowledge, intellectual endeavors. Its planetary correspondence is Mercury.

- Red: force of will, energy, courage, battle, valor, intensity, lust, passion. Its planetary correspondence is Mars.

- Pink: love, romance, friendship, relationships, happiness. Its planetary correspondence is Venus.

- Gold: healing and success. Its planetary correspondence is the sun.

- Silver: psychic development, dreamwork, uncrossing. Its planetary correspondence is the moon.

- Grey: neutralizing a bad situation, uncrossing, breaking addiction, banishing, cleansing, binding.

- White: good for all magic, particularly healing. Its planetary correspondence is moon.

Traditionally, the time of the waxing moon is good for manifesting things; the waning moon, for removing negative influences; the full moon, for all positive workings; and the dark moon, for hexing and warfetters. Just as stones and herbs have specific energy resonances, so do colors and moon phases. Some people are more sensitive to these resonances than others and thus like to include them in their work. Candle magic can be enjoyable, so have fun and experiment. I've found that candles alone can dramatically change the ambience and energy of a home or space. For would-be energy-workers, a good place to start is doing a bit of candle magic to create a welcoming, soothing environment in your workspace.

Psychic and Magical Attack

Anyone who becomes involved in energy-work or magic will eventually worry about psychic or magical attack. In most cases, the "attack" will be completely unconscious. As previously noted, most people aren't aware that their emotions have power. They aren't aware of their own internal energies, and they have sloppy control over their will. In some cases, however, the attack can be the work of a trained practitioner. Regardless, the symptoms are largely the same. Many of these symptoms are physical. Before assuming attack, please make sure you are in good health. See your doctor to rule out health issues. In the case of a legitimate attack, at least three of the following symptoms will be present:

- Unexpected and negative events in your vicinity and that of your loved ones and friends.

- Unexplained bad luck, more than can be explained by mere coincidence, in every aspect of your life: relationships, work, finances, health.

- Close calls that could easily have resulted in fatality. (For example, I know one magician who was fighting off a very strong attack. One day the attack manifested in the form of a traffic light crashing down onto his car. Had he not been properly warded and very, very skilled at shielding, he'd have been killed.)

- Exhaustion.

- Headaches.

- Lack of energy or motivation.

- Nightmares.

- An unexplained feeling of being stalked, hunted, or watched.

- General ill health coinciding with at least two of the other symptoms listed here.

- Conflict in personal and professional relationships for no apparent reason. This often occurs out of the blue and quickly escalates.

- ✤ Depression and nervous anxiety.

- ✤ Electrical problems.

- ✤ Things breaking in your general vicinity, particularly electronic equipment. (This can also happen with strongly gifted people who are emotionally upset and not shielding properly.)

- ✤ Unusual and unpleasant smells in your home or office for no logical reason.

Steps to take

Most unfocused, unconscious attacks can be easily dispelled. The following steps will take care of 99 percent of the problems you will encounter.

1. If you have a suspicion about who is attacking you, return, burn, or discard any item that you have received from that person.

2. Take a cleansing bath.

3. Clean your house thoroughly, literally and then magically.

4. Examine all your wards and personal shields. Make sure they are in top working order.

5. If you know who is attacking you, or if you have a strong suspicion, avoid all contact with this person. *Do not* accept any gifts, food, or drink from him or her.

6. Examine your aura and make sure there are no holes or tears. Cleanse it regularly.

7. If possible, take a vacation. Get away from your regular environment. This can help break the link your erstwhile opponent has to you.

8. If you are religious, make offerings to your God(s) and engage in a daily, regular prayer practice. This has surprising power.

9. Make offerings to your ancestors and any other allies you may have. Explain what is happening and ask for their direct and active protection.

10. Perform whatever uncrossings or banishing rituals you have in your arsenal.

11. Schedule an appointment with a good diviner. Obtain a full reading on the situation. It doesn't hurt to get a second opinion and to call in backup. A specialist may be able to point out something that you've missed. Don't go to a store-front psychic. Ideally, you should seek out a spirit-worker or shaman.

Three Principle Laws of Magic

Although there are many laws in the magical world, the following three are, to my mind, the most important—especially for healers, who may be the first to encounter the problems that these "laws" can create. (Note: there is no such thing as the so-called law of three. The whole Wiccan idea of "three-fold return" has no basis in magical fact. That said, there are worse ways to live one's life than by attempting to do no harm. It may not always be possible, but it's a worthy goal to have.)

The law of sympathy

This law states that like attracts like. This means that lesser objects with certain characteristics can be used to symbolize greater objects that reflect those same characteristics. Thus gold can symbolize the power of the sun, silver can symbolize the moon, salt can symbolize the earth, and water can symbolize the power of the ocean. You can also use the lesser object in place of the greater and the greater will respond according to how you treat the lesser. Thus, whatever you do to a poppet (effigy or voodoo doll), a picture of someone, or a clipping of someone's hair will affect the person that the object represents. This leads us directly to the second law.

The law of contagion

This law states that what was once a part of you always remains a part of you, and that whatever is done to the part will affect the whole in a similar fashion. This law also states that when two people are in physical contact, an etheric or astral bond is created. This is particularly important in sexual intercourse. Keep in mind that through the exchange of energy and body fluids, a powerful magical connection is being created. This is also the reason so many spells call for personal concerns such as fingernail clippings, a piece of hair, or even bodily fluids. It provides a powerful line right through a person's shields because, again, what was once a part of a person remains forever tied to him or her. Even photos can hold a certain amount of energy. Working magic with someone and performing energy-work on someone also create etheric cords.

The law of negative rebound

This law is of utmost importance in combat, attack, and, by extension, protection. This law states that if an object of an attack is too well-shielded for the attack to find its mark, it will hit the weakest point closest to the target. For instance, someone throws a magical attack at you, and instead of hitting you, it hits your cat, which dies.[7] Or instead of hitting you physically, it hits a weakness in your Wyrd and you lose your job, or your car takes the attack for you and breaks down. Sometimes, if you are wearing magically protective jewelry, the jewelry can suddenly break if it absorbs an attack. The corollary to this is that if you mount an attack and your opponent is too well-shielded or actively deflects the attack back to you, you the caster can get hit, either with backlash from the reflected spell or with negative rebound on yourself.

For those of you reading my book who are seriously contemplating finding a teacher or taking up the study of energy-work and magic, there are a couple of important factors to consider. Firstly, studying energy-work, magic, and even psi-gifts will change you. To do these things well, there is a tremendous amount of ongoing self-examination that must occur. Ultimately there really isn't a lot of room for sentimentality, and none at all for delusion or self-pity. The work will either show clear, clean, reasonably predictable results or it won't. If the internal work is done, it will either make you a more stable, more grounded, more powerful person or it will lead to delusion, addiction, and even madness. But no-one ever remains the same after embarking upon this path of study.

I am frequently asked where to find a teacher, and if there are schools or groups I can recommend. Sadly, the answer is almost always no. There are individual teachers that I can highly recommend, but they are few and far between. The majority of groups I have encountered either have no idea what they're talking about and are teaching nonsense, or are actively attempting to exploit the gifts of their students. Although the latter is, thankfully, not the norm, it can and does happen.

Most likely you will encounter very well-meaning groups that are teaching very well-meaning but dangerous nonsense. In the early stages of training, it's very easy to get sucked in, and it's very difficult to separate the proverbial wheat from the chaff—particularly when the "chaff" looks easy, pleasant, and non-threatening and promises immediate results. Many groups that focus on energy-work also focus on communicating or working with otherworldly beings, beings which are clearly not Deities. While this can be done effectively and safely, I have yet to see it in any public group. Usually there is a remarkable lack of self-preservation and security awareness. Therefore, you should avoid any group that emphasizes the following activities:

- Communing with compassionate, benevolent beings who supposedly have only one's good intentions and spiritual growth in mind.
- Focusing on "Ascended Masters."
- Working with beings devoted solely to universal goodwill and with no personal agendas of their own.

Avoid these groups like the plague. Firstly, *everything* has an agenda. Just because we can't see the agenda doesn't mean it isn't there. Secondly, most serious occultists that I know, those who are often called upon to go in and clean up other people's unfortunate messes, are of the opinion that many of those ascended masters, "benevolent" spirits, and otherworldly beings looking for people to bless with vague yet reassuring words of wisdom concerning the state of their higher selves are, in sad fact, feeding on the life-force, emotions, and energy of the people in question. Nine times out of 10, they're lower-level "bottom feeders" feeding on psychic energy—in other words, energy vampires. Someone with a psi-gift, particularly an un-trained psi-gift, is the equivalent of a five-star meal to some of these creatures. If you remember nothing else, remember this: there are no free rides. It's important to keep that in mind when doing this type of work.

Also avoid groups that seriously believe that all one needs to do in order to do effective energy-work are good intentions and white light. This is not only inaccurate and untrue, but dangerous. More to the point, any serious occultist or energy-worker is going to start to twitch when people start oozing sweet platitudes about the "highest good." Throughout history, uncountable atrocities have been committed in the name of the highest good. Those who do energy-work for the highest good are doing sloppy energy-work. Period. It's a nice moral cop-out.

I don't dispute that there are spirits who are far more experienced, intelligent, and compassionate than we are. But I think that even compassionate helping spirits are hoping to gain something by their work with responsive humans. They may not be seeking personal aggrandizement—they may be working to fulfill their own spiritual work—but they are almost certainly doing what they do to further their cause. This may or may not be our cause, and we may or may not understand this. So be wary. There is a lot of nonsense being touted as spiritual truth, and there are an awful lot of people convinced that they have a spiritual practice when all they have is self-delusion. Most of the time, it's harmless self-delusion, but not always. Be watchful, be wary. Remember the wonderful occult maxim that I mentioned previously, "as above, so below"? Therefore, it stands to reason that if there are bad and harmful things here in our world, there must also be bad and harmful things in the spirit world. It is always wise to be careful, and the techniques offered in this book are the first steps to doing just that. They will get you started in the right way, responsibly and safely.

I would also suggest doing whatever you need to do to deepen your spiritual and devotional practices. As a fairly hard-core occultist, I am often looked askance at by colleagues when I suggest to my students that they cultivate and maintain a regular prayer practice. However, I maintain that nothing offers more balance and protection than having the Gods in one's life. Having Someone bigger, stronger, older, and more powerful looking out for you is a very good thing. It also makes the self-examination necessary for any true magical practice far more fruitful. Magic and spirituality *can* go hand-in-hand.

Many ceremonialist magicians will tell you that the Gods are only thought-forms, or manifestations of our "higher selves." I say this is nonsense and hubris in its most egregious form. I will also point out that this is very likely the reason why so many ceremonial magicians self-destruct so early on. Be respectful. It costs you nothing to be respectful, not just in dealing with Gods, but in dealing with any other entities. Northern Tradition rune-master Galina Krasskova put it this way:

> The biggest caveat that I can offer is all about respect: just because it isn't what you might call a "God," doesn't mean it isn't worthy of courtesy and respect. These things cost nothing; they harm no one and may, in the long run, earn you many benefits. Certainly it is a way of demonstrating that you are a person of worth. This holds true across the board: respect and courtesy do not imply agreement and alliance. They tell the world(s) that you are an honorable human being who wasn't raised in a barn. They tell the beings of the nine worlds that you are a person on the path of wisdom. Self-control and discipline are highly valued in the other worlds and that certainly holds true amongst the Norse. Knowing how to behave rightly regardless of the company that one is in, well, that is the trait of the worthiest of the noblest of men and women. It is something to which everyone can aspire.[8]

Be respectful, but know when to hold your own. Having a patron Deity or a family of Deities to which one can turn for protection and guidance is something to consider. The caveat to this is that it requires the work of building an ongoing relationship with said God(s) or Goddess(es).

That said, I can well understand the hunger for an actual human teacher. Energy-work, psi-work, and magic can all be very confusing, especially at first. It's natural to want a teacher to come and make everything okay. Truthfully, working with a teacher can be a blessing. There is nothing like having clear, competent, caring guidance on a road that can sometimes be very frustrating. It also makes advancement that much easier because there's someone skilled to provide immediate feedback: yes, this is correct; no, that's not working, why don't you try X instead? If you are looking to find a teacher in psi-work or energy-work, I would look at trained occultists and magicians. Energy-work is taught in a far more organic manner, without much of the sentimentality that so often passes for "training" in many New Age groups. If possible, I would recommend finding someone experienced in both magic and shamanism or some form of spirit-work. I highly recommend the work of Raven Kaldera, Kenaz Filan, and Galina Krasskova for just this reason. In the Resources section, I also provide a list of books by authors whose work will help to provide guidance and a solid background of technique and common sense.

Although I recommend seeking out a magician for training, even if you have no desire to learn magic per se, this, too, comes with a certain caveat. I am old-school; I was trained one-on-one in an almost military fashion. I had a master teacher and I was the apprentice, and my job was to show up, put up, and shut up. I learned a great deal, but it was difficult. There was a pronounced hierarchy, and I was expected to conform to it without question. This can be very difficult for many of us, coming as we do from a modern society that emphasizes the questioning of all authority. Nevertheless, I trusted my teachers, and it was prayer, meditation, and ongoing discernment that helped me get through the rough patches in the working relationships. I also had teachers who were as patient as they could be when they saw me struggling with the protocol and hierarchy. It wasn't until I was a teacher of the Art myself that I truly understood why that hierarchy is so necessary, which is why I'm going to explain it to you here. Although not every magician works this way, in my opinion, those worth their salt do.

Magicians are territorial creatures. We grow more so as our power and skills increase. Working magic well takes a certain stubborn dominance of will that can lead to an incredible sensitivity toward power, territory, and boundaries. We know where the sphere of our influence ends to the centimeter and we generally don't much like others of equal power coming within 100 yards of our territory, even when it happens by our own invitation. For this reason, friendships between magicians of equal power can be rather prickly at times. Negotiating protocol between a group of master magicians can be a headache-inducing exercise in diplomacy and tact, even when all of the magicians involved are good friends (there's friendship and then there's work, after all). This is partly because magic is all about gaining and using power. I have heard politics called "the art of the possible," and in truth, I think magic fits this description even better. Those of us who reach the higher levels of practice are shaped and formed by the practice itself. If we don't start out with rather large egos, we tend to develop them over time. The difference here is that ego should be based on clearly recognized and demonstrable skill, not on arrogance and hubris. It goes with the territory, if you will excuse the pun. High-level magic can be difficult and even physically painful;

thus the master or adept develops a certain stubborn willfulness to endure and gain the upper hand. It's a side effect of the necessities of training.

I never really gave much thought to how this affects a magician's interaction with his or her students or apprentices until very recently. For the past two years I have taken something of a sabbatical from teaching (one does run the risk of burnout after awhile), and only recently have I again opened my doors to students and one erstwhile apprentice. I recently outsourced my current apprentice to another master magician for very specific training. When that magician in turn brought in a third teacher without informing me, I became quite angry. It was a violation (albeit unintentional on both our parts) of the protocol I had been taught. We're all control freaks. That, too, goes with the territory. Magicians are obsessed with controlling every aspect of their world as much as possible. Nowhere is that more pronounced than with their students. There is a certain professional, collegial courtesy, an etiquette that we maintain when dealing with another's student or apprentice. It's so easy to forget about that etiquette when dealing with a colleague who is also a close friend. Although the other magician and I had a productive discussion that resulted in my being kept in the organizational loop, which was what I'd wanted, and although I agreed that the outsourcing to a third party was right and necessary, the whole incident caused me to reevaluate how we were taught to relate to students and apprentices and what the difference between the two might be. There *are* differences, and there is a traditional dynamic, a cosmological "groove," that often comes into play here, and oh how I wish I'd realized that when I first began teaching!

Students and apprentices reading this book might find the reality of the matter a bit dismaying. Understand that the magician is bound just as strongly as the student or apprentice; there are obligations and duties on both sides. No one gets the proverbial free lunch here. Basically, students and apprentices are both physical extensions of the magician's territory or sphere of influence. Students have far more freedom than apprentices, and the magician has far fewer responsibilities to someone who is just a student (though what responsibilities there are tend to be quite binding). How tightly a magician controls the life of the student or apprentice varies from practitioner to practitioner. I tend to train the way I myself was trained, which was pretty old-fashioned and strict, though the older I get the more flexible I've become about the whole thing.

There is a reason for the strictness of the training: an apprentice is learning to wield a significant amount of power. This is not a game or an imaginary exercise. He or she is being exposed to training that can make him or her quite dangerous. It is the master's responsibility to ensure that the student develops a certain sense of ethics, discipline, and control; that he is she is not unbalanced by the training or the power; and that he/she understands the costs of as well as the difference between lawful and unlawful action. Until the magician is sure that the student isn't going to go off the deep end or egregiously misuse his/her training, it's best to keep control so that any potential problems can be nipped in the bud. I've seen students who gain a little skill and suddenly develop egos completely out of proportion to their training, and who then rush out to do stupid things that end up either getting themselves or someone else hurt or creating a mess for their teacher to clean up. The way to offset this is to maintain appropriate hierarchy, no matter how frustrating it might seem. It's not enough to have the skill; there must also be a decent level of maturity and discipline. Understanding—and respecting—the chain of command from the very beginning helps immensely with that.

It also gives the teacher the magical access and, moreover, the karmic right to lock the student down if necessary.

The magician is responsible for protecting the student or apprentice, for training him or her, for helping him/her develop his gifts, and, in some cases (I'm thinking of live-in apprentices here), of providing room and board. With apprentices, the master magician also holds any magical or spiritual debt incurred by the apprentice in those first fumbling years, thus preventing the apprentice from accruing drastically imbalanced Wyrd. In return, the apprentice or student works his/her butt off doing whatever he/she is told. That obedience is the currency with which the student pays for training. Apprenticeship takes this dynamic a step further. The apprentice is far more integrated into the magician's life and household. Whereas students are simply expected to practice, study, and not seek out external training without permission, apprentices may become the magician's errand boys, girl Fridays, housekeepers, and assistants as needed. They maintain a far closer relationship with the magician and in turn, gain far more knowledge and power. Essentially, the apprentice becomes a reservoir for the power that has been invested in him by the magician. He or she then becomes a living extension of the magician's will. Over time, the magician begins to allow the apprentice to take more and more of an active role in whatever work is being done, and to express far more individual initiative. Over time, both of these things combine to shape and prepare the apprentice for handling higher and higher levels of power. Eventually, the bond reaches its fulfillment and the apprentice goes off on his/her own with the blessings of the teacher. The only obligation that remains is that the apprentice cannot/should not use what he/she has learned against the teacher, and the teacher may call upon him/her for aid if needed. That hierarchy of respect remains.

At its worst, it can be a brutal system. At its best, it functions with military precision.

The downside occurs when expectations are not clearly set from the beginning. There is also the inevitability of transference (or counter-transference), particularly if the student or apprentice has any unresolved parental or authority issues. It's incumbent upon the magician to maintain constant objectivity with regard to the teacher-student or master-apprentice relationship. The personal should not enter into it. It's a hard road. My apprentice years were awful, but I learned a tremendous amount and I don't regret them in the least. I also learned that the hardest thing for a teacher is to know when to let go, when there is nothing more to teach. In the best relationship, the teacher learns as much from the process of teaching as the apprentice or student does. Ideally, the apprentice is the most trusted person in the magician's life. This is the person the magician is grooming to become a colleague, an equal, and maybe even a replacement. They should ultimately work together as a well-honed team. It doesn't always work out that way, but that is the ideal. Obviously this implies a great deal of trust on the part of the student.

When looking for a teacher, it's important to look not just at the work of a prospective teacher but at his or her life. As my own teacher once said, magic is not a substitute for poor lifestyle management. If things are not coming together well, if there is disaster after disaster and crisis after crisis, and if the life of the would-be teacher is in shambles, maybe it would be better to look elsewhere. Magic should make us more productive, not less, and if one's teacher isn't productive, that's a huge warning sign. I would encourage you to seek out a competent diviner and find out whether or not this is the right teacher for you. Sometimes all the factors are in alignment, but the personalities involved are just oil and water.

I'd suggest to the teacher that it is of utmost importance to have a support network, because teaching can be stressful; counter-transference is a terrible thing. I'd also strongly suggest that the teacher and student draft a written contract clearly stating obligations on both sides. This contract should be reviewed at least quarterly. It should clearly set out the non-negotiable expectations and obligations for both teacher and student. This is what they can fall back on when seemingly insurmountable problems arise.

There is a difference between someone who comes to me asking for specific training in one or two areas (such as basic energy-work) or who just takes a class from me, and a student who wants to learn the ins and outs of an esoteric art on an on-going basis but who does not, for some reason, wish to become an apprentice. I far prefer working with students, as the reciprocal obligations are few. You teach them what they've asked you to teach and let them go. The deeper and more involved a magician's work is with someone, the more obligations there are for that person's training, well-being, and safety. If an apprentice attracts the attention of some psychic bottom feeder or is being attacked by a negative spirit or otherworldly being, the magician's obligation is to protect that student. If an apprentice whom I have trained "goes bad," I'm responsible for cleaning up the mess and locking that person down, regardless of the cost to myself. The nature of the relationship allows the teacher to ferret out potential problems and instabilities. The downside is that as the apprentice progresses, he/she is well-placed to harm the teacher because he/she will know the ins and outs of the teacher's protections and has access to the teacher's workspace and tools. Clearly, there's a great degree of trust required on both sides. It also presupposes a degree of maturity and integrity on the part of the magician that, in reality, may sometimes be lacking. I see nothing wrong with asking for a trial period before entering into a master-apprentice bond because the last thing someone needs is to end up with a teacher who is cruel or unbalanced. Again, I'm not averse to actually writing up a contract with clearly defined responsibilities on both sides.

There is another side to the teacher-apprentice relationship (and to a limited degree, the teacher-student relationship) that is almost never discussed. Because the student or apprentice is so connected to the teacher, the law of negative rebound often comes into effect. We most often see this with familiars: if someone throws malicious or harmful magic at a magician, and his or her shields are too strong for the magic to affect him or her directly, it will often rebound and strike the point of greatest weakness—finances, a love relationship, a pet, their car, anything that isn't protected adequately. (It's amazing how being responsible and upfront in one's personal and professional dealings can go a long way toward preventing negative rebound!) One of the reasons that many magicians traditionally had pet familiars is that they served as an early warning system that someone was trying to attack the magician magically. Familiars will absorb attacks meant for the magician and, in worst case scenarios, will sicken and die. This protects the magician and gives warning that counter-measures must be taken. It's one of the fundamental purposes of a familiar. Likewise, a powerful attack can hit a student or apprentice before hitting the teacher or master. This is one of the primary reasons that I keep a close and watchful eye on my own students and my one apprentice: it is my duty to protect them from this eventuality. If you want to make a brutal point and weaken a magician, strike at his or her apprentice. It's rude, it's unfair, and it's a violation of traditional protocol, but it's also damned effective. It is only the right of ownership, invoked by the power of the traditional master-apprentice/teacher-student bond, that allows the master magician to adequately circumvent this danger.

None of this means that the master magician doesn't see and value the individual personality and talents of the student or apprentice. He does; in fact, he has to. It's because of who the apprentice is that the magician accepted him or her in that role in the first place. There has to be mutual respect and a certain compatibility of approach and personality for it to really work well. What I'm discussing here is the overarching dynamic in which that personal relationship rests—the bigger picture, if you will. The best teachers I've encountered are the ones who are always carefully and exquisitely aware of their duties and responsibilities, and who never take their students or apprentices for granted. It's a privilege, not a right, to take on that role. We have an obligation to be the type of teacher we ourselves would have wanted. Just use common sense, and always keep in mind that these practices are meant to enhance your life, the life you're living in the here and now. If it's not making you a more insightful, more grounded, more compassionate person, maybe you should give the approach a second thought.

I wish you, my readers, luck in your spiritual and magical endeavors. Despite my dire warnings, the study of energy-work, the honing one's psi-talents, and even the pursuit of magic can be incredibly challenging and rewarding. It opens doors of awareness and understanding that, quite literally, give you the power to change the world.

Epilogue

The study of energy-work and magic and the development of one's inborn psi-talents is an ongoing endeavor. It takes more than the simple study of established techniques; rather, it is a matter of learning to live in the world, of seeing everything through a very special filter, a filter comprised of excellence, discipline, courage, and perseverance. These form the habits that are necessary to gain competence in this field, and comprise the core traits that mindful practice develops.

This work is not without its dangers. Those who choose to focus on magic and energy-work first and foremost must always be on guard against arrogance and hubris. In many ways, the very discipline and focused will so necessary for effective practice often breeds a remarkable arrogance in practitioners. Ongoing spiritual practice and devotion can help to mitigate the worst of this, but even so, care must be taken. The student must never stop searching his or her soul, seeking out the tendrils of hubris that can so easily take root. Above all else, seek humility in all things.

Learn to live rightly and well in the world, as well. We are physical creatures meant to live in the physical world. It doesn't matter how much skill you have in magic or energy-work—if your life is falling apart or if you're reeling from one crisis to another, you will not be effective in either. It doesn't matter how much occult skill you gain if you cannot deal with real life. Magic and energy-work should not substitute for a well-lived life. Always ground yourself in reality. Don't let this work control you. It is a skill and a tool, one that you should always control.

Finally, be patient and practice. Skill isn't developed overnight. Committing to working with one's psi-talents or learning energy-work or magic is really about committing to self-development. That's not a process that stops. I strongly suggest keeping a journal to chart your progress. I still look back on the journal of my first year's training with wonder at how far I've come. Things that seemed impossibly difficult at one time now are routine for me. One thing that I would caution, however, is that these studies change a person. That change is inevitable and unpredictable. Someone who begins this study will not be at all the same person who continues after five years, or 10, or 20. It is a process of ongoing transformation most essentially of the spirit, the psyche, and the self. It is not something to undertake lightly.

This book is the culmination of nearly 20 years of teaching. My goal was to provide a simple manual for study and attainment, one that would teach the student not only the fundamentals of practice, but the means by which to progress safely. If this book has helped even one person reach that goal, my work is complete.

Notes

Preface

1. I categorize energy-work as an occult science, as I do magic (which is technically a type of energy-work).

Chapter 1

1. I've since met other energy-workers who were taught exactly the opposite. In the end, I suppose it doesn't really matter; there are good and logical arguments for both sides of the debate. I would suggest trying both, and sticking with the one that feels the most solid and comfortable.

2. It can be extremely disorienting, emotionally and energetically, when this is not the case. It can even lead to severe dysphoria (depression and general malaise).

3. For those who have suffered trauma or who deal with body-image issues, centering practice can put one in touch with one's body in a way that may be difficult or uncomfortable at first. This doesn't

mean that anything is wrong; rather, it means there are hurts that need to be addressed.

4. It is perfectly normal to feel a certain degree of sexual arousal during the grounding process, especially when you are first learning. If this happens, try not to become too distracted by it. Sexual arousal is, after all, just another form of energy. In our culture it's one of the few allowable conduits for intense energy. It's our "default setting," if you will, when dealing with energy, which is why strong spiritual bonds often read as sexual, something my teacher and I encountered regularly. In the case of grounding, it's also a case of the confluence of the physical and the energetic, as the genitals and the root chakra (which is all about survival instinct) are both involved. Clearly we're dealing with a very charged area!

5. Spiritual baths and rubdowns, wherein an ointment, salve, or liquid is rubbed over the body, are two common cleansing techniques.

6. Deity possession—common in some traditional religions, such Santeria and Voudoun, but controversial in others, such as Asatru/Heathenry—is a process by which certain people can set aside their consciousness (or allow their consciousness to be pushed aside) to allow a Deity to enter them and use their flesh and senses as though they were His or Her own for a certain amount of time. It is a very grueling experience, and it takes a certain inborn mental and psychic wiring to do it safely. For those interested in reading more on this subject, I highly recommend *Drawing Down the Spirits* by Raven Kaldera and Kenaz Filan.

7. The technique is fairly straightforward. You extend a mental "hand" into the other person's energy field and give it a push, focusing on creating a spiraling whirlpool; then you

gently guide the energy down into the ground, using that mental hand as a tool. Alternately, you can put your physical hands on the person's shoulders and extend your own energy into him or her, "catching" it and reaching down through his or her ground and into the earth. If you're a psi-vamp (see Chapter 2), you just eat the ungrounded energy. If you're not a psi-vamp, however, don't do this.

8. I recommend *The Essence of Tantric Sexuality* and *Tantra for Erotic Empowerment*, both by Mark Michaels and Patricia Johnson.

9. I received a good deal of my training from a Northern Tradition shaman. This had tremendous impact on the way in which I approach using and connecting to the various worlds. If I learned nothing else during her tutelage, I learned that it's always better to ask permission from and to be respectful of the denizens of the spirit-places in which I wish to work. Respect is never a bad thing.

10. Some people take the idea of being a tree to very creative ends and will actually try to embody the feeling of being a specific kind of tree, such as a birch, maple, or weeping willow. They incorporate that level of feeling or visualization into their grounding process. If you think this might help you, go for it. I don't think it can hurt.

11. For the sheer feeling of being grounded, I find that imagining oneself to be a mountain is even more effective than being a tree. Tree imagery is more effective for symbolizing energetic roots.

Chapter 2

1. Magic is a type of energy-work. Anything that involves sensing and using energy in any way is technically energy-work.

2. All magic is about power. All magicians take up the study of the Art because they desire power; they desire to bring their world into compliance with their desires and wills. This is perhaps the most difficult thing for aspiring magicians to admit. However, there is nothing wrong with this. The judicious practitioner is guided by the knowledge that the Wyrd-web must always remain in balance; otherwise it brings destruction to the magician. "Evil" magics warp the web of fate and existence (what Northern Traditionalists call Wyrd), but power itself is not evil. It is a tool, neither good nor bad. Evil will lie only in the intent of the caster. This is not a matter of magic, but of ethics. The wise magician aspires to the power of a god, all the while knowing that he or she is not a God. Honore de Balzac wrote that "power is not revealed by striking hard or striking often, but by striking true." This more than anything else describes the path of the magician. For more information on Wyrd, I suggest *Exploring the Northern Tradition* by Galina Krasskova, *The Well and the Tree* by Paul Bauschatz, and *Runes: Theory and Practice*, also by Krasskova.

3. Several telepaths of my acquaintance have talked about animal thoughts having a different frequency (either higher or lower, depending on the animal) from those of humans. One swore to me that any telepath could learn to communicate with animals just by learning to listen for a higher or lower frequency.

4. This is also a useful tool for healers of the mind.

5. Empathy is my primary gift as well as my primary means of communication. I actually have difficulty communicating effectively over the phone because I feel as though I am missing huge chunks of the conversation. It took me years to realize that this is because I'm primary empathic,

then kinesthetic (I read body language), then visual (hence, e-mail and letters work better for me than the phone), and only then, aural. I miss things, sometimes important points, when working solely by sound. This more than anything else taught me that for those with a strong psi-gift, that gift has to be taken into account when evaluating one's primary learning or communication modality because it will sometimes have a powerful effect.

6. Empaths are often extraordinarily sensitive to energy blockages and stagnant or diseased energies in the body.

7. This is true of psychological introverts, too. I can't say, however, that empaths are primarily introverts. I think they run the spectrum from introvert to extrovert to every shade in between. It's just that the gift often causes the empath to seek isolation out of painful necessity.

8. I have to say as an empath (and with a degree of cynicism) that we often don't do this out of any kindness or altruism. It's usually the only way we can get any peace. Indeed, because emotions are held in the body, emotional overload can cause a plethora of physical symptoms ranging in severity from massive tension and migraines to ulcers and even shock.

9. I've encountered gifted empaths who were convinced that they lacked psi-ability solely because they didn't have the sight, and every book they'd read and teacher they'd had focused almost exclusively on visual metaphors.

10. The future is never, ever set. What the pre-cog will pick up is the most likely outcome based on a variety of factors, including past behavior, past choices, emotions, and behavior in relationships. We are often creatures of habit; even when

we see the train coming right toward us, it can be very difficult to take the necessary action to avoid collision.

11. What a Northern Traditionalist would call Wyrd (causality and consequence).

12. Such a case would be an example of two complementary gifts working in unison to simulate a third, different gift.

13. I don't necessarily consider the ability to be possessed by the Gods mediumship. It is a unique gift or type of mental/ neurological wiring in and of itself. The majority of people I know who are able to handle Deity possession are not mediums.

14. In times of disaster when there are a high number of casualties, even people who lack this gift but who possess a certain sensitivity to the dead can find themselves being called upon to help spirits find their way across into the afterlife/ underworld. The tragedy of 9/11 is a perfect example: I know of several seers and empaths who ended up doing this, even though it wasn't something they were trained for, gifted in, or expecting.

15. It can be uncomfortable and even painful for an empath to be around a well-shielded person. This is due to the fact that there is an unspoken conversation going on as the empath uses his or her gift to read and verify what the other person is saying, picking up thousands of unseen, unspoken nuggets of information. He or she may also use it to subtly emphasize his or her own conversation points. When an empath encounters someone with iron-clad shields, the empath can feel as though he or she is hitting a brick wall.

Chapter 3

1. There are also magical shields, but the line between magic and energy-work is especially blurry where shielding is concerned.

2. I think this is because when we're sick, there is discomfort and also an unconscious withdrawal from those around us. I know that when I'm sick, I just want to be left alone!

3. It's also very uncomfortable as it removes a major means of communication, the primary sense through which empaths navigate and experience their world. I find that the discomfort and disorientation isn't worth the effect of the shield, but again, this is a very subjective thing.

Chapter 4

1. It should be fairly obvious from reading this that I, like many Northern Traditionalists and some magicians, am an animist. I strongly believe that people, places, and things all have (or in the case of man-made objects, can develop or house) their own spirits. This belief, based on 20 years of energy-work, strongly informs the nature of my practice and, consequently, of my teaching.

2. Choose a stone that you like and that you feel comfortable with. I don't click with every person I meet; neither do I click with every stone. Each person will find that their energies resonate best with certain kinds of stones. It's a matter of having compatible frequencies.

3. Many magicians, shamans, and energy-workers use their own blood in workings. The safest way to do this is to keep a box of diabetic lancets and alcohol swabs on hand. When blood is needed, one can then quickly and easily—and

safely—prick a finger. It's not quantity where blood is concerned, but quality and, more importantly, intent.

4. Take some care with this as there are some minor ethical concerns here. Make sure that you don't set your shields to draw on someone's personal energy or feed from someone else.

5. If you are having disturbing dreams or trouble sleeping, I would first try camphor. If that doesn't work (or if you can't tolerate the smell; some people are very sensitive to even the slightest whiff), put a glass of water by your bedside. Change it every night and only use the glass for this purpose. If that doesn't work, purchase a copy of Stephen Flowers' *Galdrabok* and draw the sigil that he calls "astros" on a piece of paper. Put a few drops of your blood on it and hang it above your bed. It is a powerful warding sigil and will slice to ribbons any beings or sentient energies that attempt to come in through your dreams.

6. How many tablespoons you use depends entirely on how strong you want the infusion to be. I like strong infusions so I usually use four tablespoons of each herb. Don't drink it, though; although it's safe and non-toxic, this mixture is not meant to be taken internally and will taste awful.

7. Not to mention the occasional astral or spectral "rider," or hanger-on.

8. This only works if you can be completely open about your energy-work or occult endeavors. If that's not the case, more subtle techniques will have to be used.

9. I've also found that many ancestral spirits like to be given bowls of water with healthy doses of Kolonia Sandalo in them. Like marjoram and basil, it's one of those tools that

can help make a home inhospitable to negative energies. It also has a very calming effect on a home's energy.

10. For the record, water works just as well. In a pinch, I've done this with nothing but the energy I've raised.

11. Many traditional protective charms include urine. There's no way around this. I haven't found an effective substitute. Basically the modern practitioner just has to deal with it and set aside any squeamishness. As a student of mine once wryly remarked, at least your pee is free.

12. I once brought out one of my witch bottles to show my students during a workshop I was holding in my apartment. Several backed away from it, none would touch it, and all were dissuaded from making one due to the way it felt energetically. It is a sinkhole for all the malignant, unpleasant, negative energy that is thrown at you or your space. These things usually feel vile. Before I touched it I swathed my hands in silk, which is an excellent energetic insulator. Even then I felt as though I'd been burned. They are nasty but incredibly effective. These charms have amazing staying power.

13. Faux silk works almost as well as the real thing when it comes to insulating against an object's energy.

Chapter 5

1. Draja Mickaharic also mentions the beer bath on pages 16–17 of his book *Spiritual Cleansing*, published in 1982 by Weiser Books.

2. I am not a practitioner of an Afro-Caribbean religion. My knowledge of the Orisha is secondary and grew out of my

occult work. No disrespect is intended to either the Orisha or Their devotees.

3. Working with these four elements predates Wicca by a significant number of years. It evolved as part of Western occultism, which has its roots in ancient Greece and was developed during the early Renaissance.

4. In Norse cosmology, for instance, the universe was created from the interplay of ice and fire.

5. See Pollington's *Leechcraft*, published in 2001 by Anglo-Saxon Books.

6. Some Wiccans and Pagans will argue that a ritual knife should be purposefully dulled. I find this absolutely offensive to warrior Deities, to the spirit of the blade, to the Art and Craft of magic, to the art and craft of bladesmithing, and to one's ancestors, who used knives for survival. Blades are sacred because of their nature: they are weapons; they are meant to cut. Dulling a blade on purpose is asinine.

7. I have a number of colleagues who practice ordeal work. This is the careful and purposeful use of pain as a tool for a specific spiritual or magical reason. I know of a case in which malignant energy had to be literally cut out of a person with a scalpel. This was a rare case, though, and the person was a magician who had been magically attacked and infected with a magical blight called "elfshot." All other methods of cleansing had failed. It goes without saying that one should not attempt this on one's own. In every case I know of, experienced ordeal workers were involved.

8. This is a very individual thing. I like to ground and center and feel that it actually provides a stability that enables me to read more effectively. Conversely, I have several colleagues who do all they can to open themselves up, actually

un-grounding in order to be receptive enough to read. It's a personal and individual thing, and only experience will show what works best for each diviner.

Chapter 6

1. How this talent manifests can vary depending on what other psi-talents one has. Although the psi-talents are neither energy-work nor magic, they do make the application of magic much easier—otherwise, it can feel as though you are working blind. There's also the fact that both magic and energy-work can open otherwise latent gifts.

2. Please see Galina Krasskova's *Runes: Theory and Practice* for more information on using blood in magic.

3. Ibid.

4. My training has, for the most part, been in Western occult traditions only. The four elements mentioned here are part of that tradition. Those working in Eastern traditions will encounter other combinations of elements forming the traditional basis of their practices. I cannot speak to those with any authority as they are outside the scope of my own training.

5. Personal communication with Galina Krasskova on February 17, 2010.

6. "Uncrossing" is a hoodoo term for a spell performed to cleanse you of all negativity or to break a hex that has been cast upon you. In this parlance, to "cross" someone is to put a spell on him or her, whereas to "uncross" is to break such a spell.

7. On the subject of pets, this particular law is of special importance. Many energy-workers and magical practitioners

have pets that they consider their special companions, allies, or familiars. In the event of a magical attack, these animals serve one purpose: as horrible as it may sound, they are the first line of defense. If an energy-worker or magician is attached to his or her pet, as most pet owners are, the pet will absorb the attack for that person. This can result in the pet becoming ill and even dying in some cases. I've lost two cats this way. That was when I stopped having pets. There's no way to prevent this, as far as I know. Pets are weak spots.

8. Quoted from *http://krasskova.weebly.com/blog.html*, accessed March 22, 2010.

Bibliography

Andrew, Ted. *Simplified Magic*. St. Paul, Minn.: Llewellyn Publications, Inc., 1997.

Bauschatz, Paul. *The Well and the Tree*. Amherst, Mass.: University of Massachusetts Press, 1982.

Beyerl, Paul. *The Master Book of Herbalism*. Custer, Wash.: Phoenix Publishing Company, 1984.

Coleman, Martin. *Communing with Spirits*. York Beach, Maine: Samuel Weiser, Inc., 1998.

Cunningham, Scott. *Crystal, Gem, and Metal Magic*. St. Paul, Minn.: Llewellyn Publications, Inc., 1996.

Denning, Melita, and Osborne Phillips. *Practical Guide to Psychic Self-Defense*. St. Paul, Minn.: Llewellyn Publications, 2002.

Fortune, Dion. *Esoteric Orders and Their Work*. York Beach, Maine: Samuel Weiser, Inc., 2000.

———. *Psychic Self-Defense*. York Beach, Maine: Samuel Weiser, Inc., 1997.

———. *The Training and Work of an Initiate*. York Beach, Maine: Samuel Weiser, Inc., 2000.

Gray, William. *Exorcising the Tree of Evil.* Cape Town, South Africa: Kima Global Publishers, 2002.

Hope, Murray. The World of Psychism. Leicestershire, UK: Thoth Publications, 2001.

Kaldera, Raven, and Tannin Schwartzstein, Tannin. *The Urban Primitive.* St. Paul, Minn.: Llewellyn Publications, Inc., 2002. (An updated reprint is forthcoming from Asphodel Press.)

———. *The Ethical Psychic Vampire.* Bloomington, Ind.: Xlibris, 2005.

———. *Pathwalkers' Guide to the Nine Worlds.* Hubbardston, Mass.: Asphodel Press, 2007.

———. *Wightridden: Techniques of Northern Tradition Shamanism.* Hubbardston, Mass.: Asphodel Press, 2007.

———. *Wyrdwalkers: Techniques of Northern Tradition Shamanism.* Hubbardston, Mass.: Asphodel Press, 2007.

King, Francis, and Stephen Skinner. *Techniques of High Magic.* Rochester, Vt: Destiny Books, 2000.

Krasskova, Galina. *Exploring the Northern Tradition.* Franklin Lakes, N.J.: New Page Books, 2005.

———. *Runes: Theory and Practice.* Franklin Lakes, N.J.: New Page Books, 2009.

Mauss, Marcel. *A General Theory of Magic.* Oxford, UK: Routledge, 2006.

Michaels, Mark, and Patricia Johnson. *The Essence of Tantric Sexuality.* St. Paul, Minn.: Llewellyn Publications, Inc., 2006.

———. *Tantra for Erotic Empowerment.* St. Paul, Minn.: Llewellyn Publications, Inc., 2008.

Mickaharic, Draja. *Practice of Magic.* York Beach, Maine: Samuel Weiser, Inc., 1995.

———. *Spiritual Worker's Spellbook.* York Beach, Maine: Samuel Weiser, Inc., 2002.

———. *Magical Techniques.* Bloomington, Ind.: Xlibris, 2002.

———. *Magical Influence.* Bloomington, Ind.: Xlibris, 2002.

Nema. *The Way of Mystery.* St. Paul, Minn.: Llewellyn Publications, Inc., 2003.

Regardie, Israel. *The Middle Pillar.* St. Paul, Minn.: Llewellyn Publications, Inc., 1978.

———. *The One-Year Manuel: Twelve Steps to Spiritual Enlightenment.* York Beach, Maine: Samuel Weiser, Inc., 1981.

Thorsson, Edred. *Futhark.* York Beach, Maine: Samuel Weiser, Inc., 1984.

———. *Runelore.* York Beach, Maine: Samuel Weiser, Inc., 1987.

Yronwode, Catherine. *Hoodoo Herb and Root Magic.* Forestville, Calif.: Lucky Mojo Publishing, 2002.

Recommended Blogs and Websites

The Gods' Mouths: *godsmouths.blogspot.com.*

Blood for the Divine: *bloodfordivine.blogspot.com.* (This journal focuses specifically on ordeal work and may contain disturbing images and/or articles.)

Catharine Yronwode's hoodoo and root-work course, offered at *www.luckymojo.com.*

Gangleri's Grove, the personal Website of rune-worker and shaman Galina Krasskova: *krasskova.weebly.com/blog.html.*

Raven Kaldera's Website on Northern Tradition shamanism: *www.northernshamanism.org.*

Author Kenaz Filan's Website and blog offers excellent articles on a variety of occult topics: *kenazfilan.blogspot.com.*

Index

About the Author

Sophie Reicher has been an occultist and magician for more than 20 years. Originally trained in ceremonial magic, she has also studied Kabala, hoodoo/rootwork, and rune magic. She is a regular contributor to two online magazines: *godsmouths.blogspot.com* and *bloodfordivine.blogspot.com*. Her work may also be found in *Day Star and Whirling Wheel* and *Runes: Theory and Practice*, both by Galina Krasskova. Reicher can frequently be found teaching classes in basic psychic protection in New York City, where she lives and works.